75 x Lace

Patricia Wardle

WAANDERS PUBLISHERS

RIJKSMUSEUM, AMSTERDAM

Foreword

This year the Rijksmuseum is celebrating the 75th anniversary of the Eerste Nederlandsche Vereeniging van Kantliefhebbers 'Het Kantsalet' with an exhibition of 75 prime pieces from the lace collection. It is to the generosity of Het Kantsalet, one of the regulations of which at its foundation was to enrich the collection of lace of the Rijksmuseum, that the museum owes many of its masterpieces.

The foundation of the lace collection was laid in the Nederlandsch Museum van Geschiedenis en Kunst, which also included the Koninklijk Kabinet van Zeldzaamheden. Most of the pieces there had presumed associations with leading historical figures. In the new Rijksmuseum (1885) these collections were amalgamated with loans from the Koninklijk Oudheidkundig Genootschap, which also possessed lace. During this period the collection grew only slowly, mainly through gifts. This is remarkable in view of the fact that at the end of the 19th century a start had been made in museums at various places abroad on the systematic acquisition or augmentation of lace collections. Only in 1920 did such a development begin in the Rijksmuseum.

The driving force proved to be Louise Wilhelmina (Mien) van der Meulen-Nulle, former bobbin lace teacher at the Rijksschool voor Kunstnijverheid, who took on the task of washing and cataloguing the collection. This enabled her to point out the gaps in it and she was soon given permission to fill them. Fortunately, knowledge of the existing collection also grew at the same time thanks to the presence of lace in the permanent display. However, this resulted only in sporadic gifts, while there was a total lack of purchasing funds in the Rijksmuseum. This led in 1925 to the foundation in Amsterdam of the Eerste Nederlandsch Vereeniging van Kantliefhebbers 'Het Kantsalet'.

Naturally, Mien van der Meulen was one of the founders, who otherwise consisted of wealthy Amsterdam ladies. In 1926 Het Kantsalet organized its first lace exhibition in the Rijksmuseum. This caused its fame and membership to grew to the extent that the first gifts to the museum could be effected. From that moment on Het Kantsalet was to offer virtually each year one or more pieces of lace to the Rijksmuseum's collection. Nor did its individual members fail to follow suit and give generously. Masterpieces like an alb flounce of *point de France* of the first quarter of the 18th century or a Chinoiserie flounce of Argentan needle lace (1725-1735) and a *blonde* silk bobbin lace scarf (1825-1835) all came from or via Het Kantsalet.

The growing importance of the Rijksmuseum's lace collection led in 1966 to the long-term loan of lace from the royal collection. Queens Emma and Wilhelmina, both great lovers of lace, had acquired or been given exceptionally costly and interesting pieces. This collection completed the holdings of lace already in the Rijksmuseum to such an extent that from that moment on it was possible to display a fine survey of the developments in lace from the Renaissance to the early part of the 20th century.

Over the last 75 years the Rijksmuseum has been able to reap the benefit of Het Kantsalet's determination to enrich its lace collection. May this publication and exhibition serve to evince the Rijksmuseum's close links with and gratitude to Het Kantsalet for its tireless dedication.

Professor Ronald de Leeuw
Director General

Lace in the Rijksmuseum

Lace has always figured prominently in the Rijksmuseum in paintings, particularly those of the 17th century, but it took a long time for it to be adequately represented in its own right as a textile. One of the reasons for this may have been that, while lace was certainly made in the Northern Netherlands from the second half of the 16th century onwards, the industry was only a minor one, certainly by comparison with those in the Southern Netherlands, France or Italy. This may also help to explain why lace collecting in general was quite slow in getting under way here by comparison with elsewhere. Nevertheless, by the time the Nederlandsch Museum van Geschiedenis en Kunst (Netherlands Museum of History and Art) was transferred to the new Rijksmuseum building in 1883, some lace had already found its way into the collection.

Het Nederlandsch Museum van Geschiedenis en Kunst in The Hague

Before it came to Amsterdam, the Nederlandsch Museum, founded in 1876, had been housed in a building on Prinsengracht in The Hague. The nucleus of its collection came from the Koninklijk Kabinet van Zeldzaamheden (Royal Cabinet of Curios), which had been in the Mauritshuis since 1821. Among the relics of the House of Orange in the collection was a lace-trimmed shirt said to have been worn by King-Stadholder William III (1650-1702) 'during the three last days of his life, after his fatal fall from his horse,' but which is more likely to have belonged to his father William II (1626-1650) or to William Frederick of Nassau-Dietz (1613-1664).[1] This had been joined in 1875 by two lace collars or bibfronted bands, one of needle lace (cat. no. 23), the other of bobbin lace. One of them was simply described as 'An old collar of lacework, formerly in use among Gentlemen' in the guide to the Mauritshuis, but they both later acquired the status of relics of William III, simply because of their juxtaposition in the register next to another relic.[2] One of various pieces of a black lace-trimmed cloak said to have been worn by the statesman and jurist Hugo de Groot (1583-1645), which was given to the museum in 1887, has likewise since been discounted, though it has undoubted value as a rare surviving example of 17th-century black silk lace.[3]

The first acquisition of lace as such, rather than as a relic or costume item, came in 1879 with the purchase of 'a remarkable collection of lacework, consisting of 29 pieces of various techniques, patterns and sizes' for the not inconsiderable sum of ƒ350, which was justified by the director in his letter to the minister as follows, 'Since the commercial value is higher and the Museum possesses no lacework at all as yet, this purchase is much to be recommended'.[4] Most of these pieces were Flemish 17th-century bobbin lace, such as had been widely used in the Northern Netherlands. Their acquisition marked the beginning of the Rijksmuseum's lace collection and the fact that they were given numbers embroidered by hand in red cross stitch can be taken as a sign of the value placed on them.

Het Koninklijk Oudheidkundig Genootschap

The new Rijksmuseum building also offered a home for the collections of the Koninklijk Oudheidkundig Genootschap (Royal Antiquarian Society), which had been founded in 1858 for the express purpose of preserving the national heritage. Lace from this source too came into the Nederlandsch Museum's collection. It included the inevitable relic in the shape of two pillow covers with the cutwork and bobbin lace said to have come from the estate of Admiral Michiel de Ruyter (1607-1676).[5] There was also a lace pillow[6] and a curious selection of lace from the estate of the history painter Nicolaas Pieneman (1809-1860). This included a piece of German *lacis*, a fine Dutch *lacis* cloth of 1623 (cat. no. 6), both rather comically catalogued as 'antimacassars', and a very odd array of collars and cuffs composed of 17th-century laces of different periods, which may have provided inspiration for Pieneman's paintings.[7]

The Nederlandsch Museum in the new Rijksmuseum building

In the Nederlandsch Museum's display of applied art, which was opened to the public in stages from 1886 onwards, many of the objects were shown in 'period rooms'. In the guide compiled by the director, David van der Kellen Jr (1827-1895), Room 154 with two sets of wood panelling of the first half of the 17th century was described as having 'something downright homely and cosy' about it, thanks to its furnishings. These included a lace pillow, 'which the lady of the house has just abandoned for a moment,' an object which had been bought in 1881.[8] Otherwise the only item with lace mentioned is the shirt associated with William III, shown in Room 152, which was 'largely devoted to historical memen-

1 Kasteele n.d., no. 742; Kellen 1879, p.4; Wardle 1992, p. 4; Kist 1995, p. 34.
2 Kellen n.d., no. 705; Erkelens 1955, fig. 14; Wardle 1992, fig. 8; Baart 1995, p. 35.
3 Wardle 1985, pp. 212-215.

4 *Jaarverslag* 1879, p. 43; the letter, dated 29 August 1879, Archief van het Rijksmuseum, no. 963.
5 Kellen 1876, nos. 934-935.
6 Ibid., no. 369.
7 Ibid. nos. 370-373, 375, 376.
8 Kellen n.d., pp. 115-116.

tos'.[9] Later on lace was also to be seen in the display of costume and textiles opened in the 'Western Pavilion' in 1889.

However, interest in lace collecting in the Rijksmuseum was to be at a decidedly low ebb for the remainder of the 19th and the first two decades of the 20th century and the same applied to knowledge of lace. In his introduction to a book recording the lace exhibition at the Museum van Kunstnijverheid (Museum of Applied Art) in Haarlem in 1903 the director, Edouard A. von Saher (1849-1918), wrote that 'only a few are as yet familiar with laces, can distinguish their various sorts correctly and have a knowledge of their techniques', the exhibition having been mounted in an effort to remedy this.[10] Each year in the Nederlandsch Museum an item or two, generally lace-trimmed costume accessories, trickled in, mostly as a gift. 1905 saw the purchase of an important linen cover with embroidery, *lacis* and bobbin lace, the arms of Poll, Pieck and Balveren and the date 1635,[11] but the only other sizable purchase of the period had been that of 1892, when ƒ350 was paid for a series of objects bought by the Amsterdam dealer J. Boas Berg from the Oud-Katholieke Kerk (Old Catholic Church) in the city on condition that they would be offered to the Nederlandsch Museum. They included what was described as an important collection of 'Dutch lace'.[12] It is doubtless illustrative of the general state of knowledge in the museum at that time that almost all the pieces are actually Venetian-type flat needle or tape laces, while the general lack of interest in lace is confirmed by the fact that after 1879 there was not a single mention of it in the museum's annual reports until 1920.

Lace collecting in the 19th and early 20th centuries
This lukewarm approach is surprising at a period when in other countries private individuals and museums were avidly engaged in lace collecting. In the Netherlands this activity seems to have been confined to royal and aristocratic circles at this time. Both Queen Emma (1858-1934)[13] and Queen Wilhelmina (1880-1962) had a great fondness for lace and an interest in acquiring antique pieces, although not on any very large scale or systematic basis. Both of them lent lace old and a new to an exhibition in The Hague in 1912 and Queen Emma also to one in Amsterdam in the same year.[14] Most of the other lenders were either aristocratic ladies, some of them, like Baroness De Constant Rebecque, close to court circles, or people with a direct involvement with

the Koninklijke Nederlandsche Kantwerkschool (Royal Dutch Lace School) in The Hague. It was, however, pointedly remarked in the Amsterdam catalogue that lace was a 'beautiful but so little known expression of art industry'. On this evidence there were no collections in the Netherlands at this time of a systematic character, like that of Flemish lace acquired by Augusta, Baroness Leids (1850-1885), which was donated to the Gruuthuse Museum in Bruges after her death,[15] or of the extent of the 400 or so pieces left to the Musées Royaux d'Art et d'Histoire in Brussels by Madame Montefiore in 1894.[16] In a perceptive discussion of lace collecting published in Paris in 1930, it was stated that the majority of the great collectors were at the same time either lace manufacturers or lace merchants.[17] The manufacturer in particular, it was pointed out, started collecting in order to have on hand copious rich documentation providing inspiration on which to draw for new designs, but then fell under the spell of the lace and turned to collecting it as an art object. This was certainly true of the French manufacturer Alfred Lescure (1862-1913), who was credited with having single-handedly brought about the revival of lace in the Auvergne[18] and whose superb collection,[19] though now scattered, is still recalled by fine pieces in various museums, the Rijksmuseum included (cat. nos. 1, 29). Another impassioned manufacturer-collector was Léopold Iklé (1838-1922), the son and joint-successor of the founder of one of the leading machine-embroidery firms at St. Gallen in Switzerland.[20] He, indeed, began by collecting lace and embroidery as models, donating his collection to the Industrie- und Gewerbemuseum in St. Gallen (now the Textilmuseum) in 1901.[21] He had become so fascinated by these textiles, however, that he immediately embarked upon a second collection, which passed on his death to his son Fritz (Friedrich Arnold, 1877-1946). Two pieces from this collection are now in the Rijksmuseum (cat. nos. 4, 21).

The collection of the museum at St. Gallen was specifically intended as an adjunct of the design school and machine-embroidery industry there, while various other museums, most notably the Victoria & Albert Museum in London, also began with the improvement of art industry as a primary aim. One of these, which began collecting lace in 1887, was the Danske Kunstindustrimuseum in Copenhagen, which in 1887

9 Ibid., p. 117.
10 Naber 1903, Introduction.
11 Burgers 1990(1), p. 54, fig. 14.
12 Archief van het Rijksmuseum, no. 976, letter of 9 March 1892.
13 Wardle 1998, pp. 25-26.

14 Kunstzaal Kleykamp Oude Scheveningseweg 3, The Hague March 1912; Larensche Kunsthandel, Herengracht 495, Amsterdam May 1912.
15 *Anciennes Dentelles* 1889.
16 Overloop 1911-1912, introduction.
17 Magué 1930, p. 6.
18 *Exposition de Bruxelles* 1910, p. 10.
19 Cox 1908; Van Overloop 1914.
20 Graff-Hofgen 1976. I am indebted to Dr Anne Wanner-JeanRichard for details on Iklé.
21 Iklé & Fäh n.d.

and 1907 bought a number of pieces from Julius von Kaan, a Munich dealer.[22] He also approached the Nederlandsch Museum in 1894, offering antique Italian lace for sale, but his overtures met with no response.[23] Both the St. Gallen and Copenhagen museums collected prime examples of Art Nouveau lace in the early years of the 20th century, but this was something entirely outside the Nederlandsch Museum's remit at that time, with the result that this important aspect of the history of lace is now represented in the collection only by loans (cat. nos. 72, 73, 75).

In the last decades of the 19th century lace collecting had also got under way in the United States, where in 1879 a first donation of a collection of lace was made to the Metropolitan Museum of Art in New York, other gifts and bequests following in the 1880s and 1890s. Other museums in New York and elsewhere also began collecting around this time, while a great stimulus was provided in 1893 by an exhibition at the Chicago World's Fair organized by a committee of New York women.[24] Among the collections represented there were those of the second wife and daughter of the wealthy banker J. Pierpont Morgan (1837-1913), while another collector in the family was Morgan's sister, Mary Lyman Morgan (1844-1919, later Mrs Walter Burns), whose collection, which passed to her daughter in England, contained many fine pieces. They included a famous *point de France* flounce acquired for the Rijksmuseum in 1980 (cat. no. 20).[25] A steady increase in donations to their collections in the first decades of the 20th century meant that by 1920 American museums possessed 'storehouses of treasures...exquisite craftsmanship developed in an age unhampered by the rush and turmoil of modern life.'[26]

The turning point
The turning point for the lace collection in the Nederlandsch Museum came in 1920. In November 1918 Marinus van Notten (1875-1955), who had been appointed director in January that year, had written to the Minister of Education, Art and Sciences asking permission for ten pieces of lace, which had become badly foxed, to be washed.[27] In 1920 it was decided to have the whole collection washed in preparation for the projected new display of costume and lace and this time the person commissioned to do the job and also to catalogue

the lace was the redoubtable Mrs Louise Wilhelmina (Mien) van der Meulen-Nulle (1884-1982) (fig. 5). The former head of the Koninklijke Nederlandsche Kantwerkschool in The Hague and after that teacher of bobbin lace at the Rijksschool voor Kunstnijverheid (National Applied Art School) adjacent to the Rijksmuseum building, Mien van der Meulen also had a keen interest in antique lace. She had helped with the exhibition in The Hague in 1912 and organized the one that followed in Amsterdam, at both of which pieces from royal collections were shown. After a spell in the Dutch East Indies she had returned to the Netherlands in 1918 and embarked on the next stage of her career, in which she single-handedly set about arousing interest in lace in the country. This she did not only by giving private lessons in lace-making, but also by lecturing on the techniques and history of antique lace, washing and repairing it and later also dealing in it from her home in Apeldoorn.[28]

Having duly washed and catalogued the collection, Mien van der Meulen made it plain in a letter of 7 September 1920 that she considered it a totally inadequate representation: 'With regard to the supplementing of the collection, I present the following for your consideration. Types of lace of which there are few or no specimens present are point de France, point de Sedan, point de Burano, point d'Argentan, point d'Alençon, point de Bruxelles; Bruxelles called Angleterre, Mechlin, Valenciennes, Honiton and all the modern types of lace. The old types could be added in the following objects: *Coiffures* with lappets, cravats, *tabliers* and sleeve ruffles, all 18th and 19th century, as well as lace worn by priests and for church use. All these objects would at the same time supplement the costume collection and thus complete the museum collections in two departments.'[29]

After that what could Van Notten do but agree to Mien van der Meulen's further suggestion that she personally assist with the enlargement of the collection. In early October 1920 she arranged for a selection of lace to be sent by a dealer of the name of Moens of Rue de Marquis in Brussels. Eighteen pieces of mostly 18th-century lace were acquired for the museum from this consignment, seven from a second in the same year. 'In this way,' Van Notten wrote in his annual report, 'a small collection has been formed, which can now already provide a survey of the various patterns and techniques used in making lace.'[30] He further noted that this had been achieved 'through friendly assistance from well-disposed persons who several times also lent financial sup-

22 Paludan et al, 1991, pp. 7, 10, 35-36.
23 Archief van het Rijksmuseum, no. 978.
24 For all this see Morris & Hague 1926.
25 I am indebted to Christine Nelson of the Pierpont Morgan Library for details of the family.
26 Morris & Hague 1926, p. 20.
27 Archief van het Rijksmuseum, no. 1002, letter of 25 November.

28 Rogge 1923, p. 31.
29 Archief van het Rijksmuseum, no. 1004.
30 Jaarverslag 1920, p. 18.

port.' That support was to lead in only a few more years to the founding of Het Kantsalet.

The first comprehensive display

In March 1921 the journalist Elisabeth (Elis) Rogge gave an account of the recent growth of the collection at the beginning of a comprehensive review of the new display of lace, which was arranged in six cases in the costume gallery and a small adjacent room.[31] The first case contained various types of *lacis* and whitework, the armorial piece of 1635 being hung on the wall of an adjacent corridor. The two cases in the costume gallery were devoted to needle lace and here Elis Rogge waxed particularly enthusiastic over the large piece of 'Alençon' needle lace, which at ƒ800 had been one of the most expensive purchases from Moens. Acquired as 'Burano in imitation of Alençon, 18th century', it is actually a piece made at the revived lace school in Burano in the late 19th century. Rogge also noted the complete absence of *point de France*. Bobbin lace was arranged by types in three cases in the small room, but here some of the cases were so crowded that individual pieces could not be seen properly. Rogge remarked that the director had given much thought to the desirability of showing 'such costly works of decorative art in the most literal meaning of the word' in rather old cases in such a small space, but in the end this had been done 'in the firm conviction that the viewing and enjoyment of so much beautiful work will arouse the interest and love of many, in whose possession so many pieces of lace of the good period are still to be found,' the long-term aim being to achieve 'a better exhibition of, it is to be hoped, a by then totally complete, historical lace collection in a gallery specially built for it.' She concluded by expressing the hope that many people would go to see the lace and be inspired to help with the expansion of the collection.

That hope had already begun to be realized even before she wrote those words. In connection with the display Mien van der Meulen had given two series of four lectures on lace,[32] as a result of which H.C. Rehbock had offered a collection of lace. A selection of 18th-century pieces (cat.no. 48) was made from this and some of them were added to the new display.[33] In 1921 a further gift, described in the annual report as 'very important', was forthcoming from Jonkheer and Jonkvrouw Baroness van Lynden-van Hemmen. This again was mostly 18th-century lace, which presumably came from a family collection. Further acquisitions were made in the early twenties by means of exchanges of 'duplicates' or even of

portions of pieces in the collection. Mien van der Meulen herself participated in the exchange process and arranged a few more purchases, one of them partly financed by one of her pupils. In 1922 some of the items in the collection were lent to an exhibition at the Friesch Museum in Leeuwarden[34] and in 1924 the lace display was changed. The cases, now stationed among the costumes, were rearranged and some of the lace was actually shown on the costumes, while portraits were also added to the display.[35] During the opening two Brussels lace cravats were donated by Mr and Mrs J.C.J. Drucker-Fraser, great benefactors of the Rijksmuseum in respect of 19th-century paintings.[36]

All this was encouraging, but the acquisition of large pieces still presented problems. Elis Rogge noted in 1921 that she was shown a fine piece of *point de France*, which could not be acquired because of a lack of funds.[37] Finally, early in 1925 it was decided that something must be done about this.

The founding of Het Kantsalet

In a letter of 28 November 1925 to the Minister of Education, Art and Sciences the director, now Frederik Schmidt-Degener (1881-1941), who had taken over responsibility for the decorative arts in 1924 after becoming Director-General of the Rijksmuseum in 1922, stated that 'A committee of ladies with good intentions towards our collection of antique lace in the Rijksmuseum has come into being to expand our collection by gifts from time to time'.[38] This 'committee' had in

fig. 1 Caricatures of Nellie Hudig and Johanna van Nierop made by Ina Schoch in July 1938 for the silver jubilee of Frederik Schmidt-Degener. Archief van het Rijksmuseum

31 Rogge 1921.
32 Jaarverslag 1920, p. 20.
33 Archief van het Rijksmuseum, no. 1004.
34 Catalogus Leeuwarden 1922, p. 22, no. 4.
35 Jaarverslag 1924, p. 18.
36 Ibid., p. 19.
37 See note 31.
38 Archief van het Rijksmuseum, Verwerving gegevens no. 220.

fig. 2 Part of Het Kantsalet's exhibition of 1926 in the rooms of the Koninklijk Oudheidkundig Genootschap. Archief van het Rijksmuseum

fact held its first meeting on 30 March 1925 at the home of one of the prime movers behind the project, Miss Johanna Elisabeth van Nierop (1882-1970) (fig. 1 right), one of Mien van der Meulen's pupils,[39] who became the first president of Het Kantsalet. The other two prime movers must have been Mien van der Meulen and Miss Cornelia (Nellie) Johanna Hudig (1879-1960) (fig. 1 left), who had joined the museum as a volunteer in March 1920 and been made an official assistant in May the following year.[40] By the time of the first meeting 27 members had already been recruited, twenty of whom were present.[41] The full name of the society was De Eerste Nederlandsche Vereeniging voor Kantliefhebbers (The First Dutch Society for Lace-lovers) 'Het Kantsalet', *salet* being an old-fashioned term for a gathering in a salon. The first meeting was held at Johanna van Nierop's house, but thereafter Het Kantsalet met in the rooms of the Koninklijk Oudheidkundig Genootschap in the Rijksmuseum.

At that first meeting the regulations of the society were read out. Its aim was 'to awaken and sustain an interest in lace', which was to be achieved by the giving of lectures on lace, by organizing exhibitions and 'by enriching the lace collection of the Rijksmuseum in Amsterdam'. Already on that very first occasion Mien van der Meulen showed the members a piece of 18th-century Brussels lace, which was to be Het Kantsalet's first gift to the Rijksmuseum (cat. no. 33).

Het Kantsalet was also immediately given an opportunity to deploy the second of its methods for promoting a love of lace, Schmidt-Degener inviting it to put on an exhibition in the Rijksmuseum. Plans for this were already discussed at a committee meeting on 1 July and the exhibition, organized in collaboration with the Koninklijk Oudheidkundig Genootschap, was held in the first three weeks of March 1926 (fig.2). It attracted nearly 3,000 visitors and was counted a great success. By the end of 1927 membership of the society had grown from 27 to 60. Clearly Het Kantsalet had got off to a flying start. That year it presented the Rijksmuseum with a cravat end of Venetian needle lace (cat. no. 21), while the first gift from a member of the society to the museum came in the shape of a blonde dress from Mrs M.E.E. Wertheim-Hijmans and a number of other gifts were made as a result of the exhibition (cat. no. 45).

Het Kantsalet had certain features in common with two earlier societies. Les Amis de la Dentelle had been founded in Brussels in 1910 in an effort to help the failing lace industry and during the First World War its members had been instrumental, in collaboration with an American committee, in keeping the lacemakers going by providing materials and new designs. When this kind of task became redundant after the war, however, Les Amis focussed their attention on the Musées Royaux d'Art et d'Histoire. Lucie Paulis, their teacher of design, was moved to the museum in 1924, where she instituted a series of lectures on the history of lace and eventually became curator of the collection, half her salary being paid by Les Amis.[42] The second precedent for Het Kantsalet, the Needle and Bobbin Club, was founded in New York in 1916. It had a somewhat wider remit: 'to encourage and maintain interest in hand-made fabrics; to promote these industries in the United States; to afford opportunities to meet and discuss lace or allied subjects'.[43] Lace was, however, a prime interest of the club's founder and first president, Gertrude Whiting, and its vice-president, Marian Hague, and in March 1917 it mounted its first exhibition, of Binche and Valenciennes lace, which was soon followed by others, including one in the Metropolitan Museum of Art in 1919. The club also provided two travelling exhibitions of lace and on the Metropolitan Museum's 50th anniversary in 1920 it donated an early 18th-century flounce of Brussels bobbin lace.[44] Het Kantsalet can, therefore, be seen as

39 A bill for lessons in 1925 is to be found among the notes of Johanna van Nierop in the Rijksmuseum.
40 Jaarverslag 1920, p. 18, 1921, p. 23.
41 Unless otherwise stated, details regarding Het Kantsalet are taken from the society's minute books and other records.

42 Coppens 1985.
43 Bulletin of the Needle and Bobbin Club, vol. I, no. 1, December 1916, p. 20.
44 Ibid., vol. I, no. 1, June 1917, pp.3-10; Vol. III, no. 2, October 1919, pp. 2-15.

part of quite a general trend at this period, and though it could not boast resources on the scale of those of the other two societies, it was certainly equally successful in pursuing its aims.

Kantsalet gifts around 1930

In 1931 Het Kantsalet was at last able to present the Rijksmuseum with the longed-for piece of *point de France*. This was all the more gratifying because in 1928 it had had to reject a similar flounce owing to lack of funds. The flounce given in 1931 (cat. no. 29) was also expensive, but as the Musées Royaux d'Art et d'Histoire were also keen on it, it was simply cut in two, a procedure often indulged in by dealers in the past. At ƒ 2,900 this was the most expensive gift made by Het Kantsalet in the years between the war. It was followed in 1933 by an almost equally expensive donation, that of a *reticella* collar, which long remained the most famous piece in the collection and figures on one of the Rijksmuseum's most striking posters (fig. 3), but which has recently proved to be a 19th-century concoction.[45] This mistake was a pardonable one, since it is only relatively recently that it has come to be realized exactly how much antique lace was remodelled in the 19th century, a practice still not entirely unknown today.

Individual members of Het Kantsalet also made gifts to the museum, most notably Mrs M.W.G. de Visser-Roelofs, who in 1930 presented thirteen pieces. All this naturally helped to create an atmosphere in which it became more common for people in general to donate or bequeath lace to the museum, particularly generous gifts being made in 1929 by the heirs of Jonkvrouw Baroness Lynden-van Hemmen and throughout the thirties by Miss G.W. Vonck (cat. no. 40).

Exhibitions and permanent display

In 1931 Het Kantsalet was invited by the Koninklijk Oudheidkundig Genootschap to assist with the organization in the Rijksmuseum of an exhibition on the Dutch interior in the 18th century. Het Kantsalet's committee members, plus Mien van der Meulen, constituted the executive committee and 28 members enthusiastically participated by lending pieces.[46] Het Kantsalet was even instrumental in arranging a musical evening on 10 April in connection with the exhibition,[47] thus inaugurating a tradition that has been continued in some of its exhibitions since the Second World War.

In October 1932 members of Het Kantsalet were informed that 'the collection of lace in the Rijksmuseum

fig. 3 Poster of 1966 by Dick Elffers, showing the *reticella* collar given by Het Kantsalet in 1933.

has become so important that this year a new room has been made available for showing it'. Many of the cases, it was stated, were still waiting to be filled, but it was hoped that this would spur members on to continue their efforts.

In April 1934 a selection of Italian lace, including pieces from the Rijksmuseum's collection, was shown in the exhibition of 'Old Italian art' in the Stedelijk Museum in Amsterdam.[48] This selection, which naturally included the standing collar given by Het Kantsalet the year before, was made by Kantsalet member Mrs O. C. D. Idenburg-Siegenbeek van Heukelom in collaboration with Nellie Hudig.

The study collection

Johanna van Nierop remained president of Het Kantsalet until the end of 1931. Several years before that, however, in 1928, she had started to work as a volunteer

---

45 An article on the collar will appear in Bulletin van het Rijksmuseum 48 (2000) no.1.
46 See cat. nos. 43-59 in Het Hollandsche Interieur 1931.
47 Archief van het Rijksmuseum, no. 2294.

48 Oud-Italiaansche Kunst 1934, cat. nos. 1182, 1203.

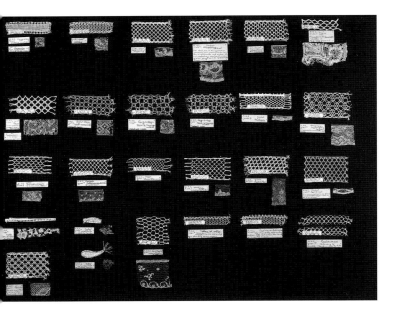

fig. 4 Frame from the former lace study collection with enlarged examples of bobbin lace techniques made by Johanna van Nierop alongside small examples of the respective laces.

on the lace collection in the Rijksmuseum, which under the rearrangement of 1927 now came under the new sculpture and decorative art section. Such was her energy and application that in the annual report of 1929 it was stated, 'Through her great dedication it has been possible for the lace in the study store to be classified and the types of lace affixed to frames made for the purpose with informative descriptions. Thus students and those interested can obtain a complete survey of the history of lace in various periods and countries. To facilitate study Miss van Nierop has made large-scale examples of needle and bobbin lace and placed these enlarged meshes next to the original old pieces' (fig. 4).[49] What is not mentioned here, is that the explanatory labels had all been written by Johanna van Nierop herself in minute, neat handwriting and that the labels as well as the lace were actually sewn to the background. Many of the examples of lace, particularly the 20th-century specimens from various countries, had also been supplied by Johanna van Nierop and her sister the economic historian Dr Leonie van Nierop (1879-1960), who shared her interest in the textile.

They continued to present samples of this type to 'this unique, informative collection, which is often consulted',[50] until 1938, when it was announced in the annual report that 'the Textile Department suffered a very

grievous loss through the departure for America of Miss J.E. van Nierop, who saw herself compelled to take leave of the work she had disinterestedly done on the Rijksmuseum's behalf for many years. The unique study collection of types of lace will continue to bear witness to her devotion and precision and likewise serve as a lasting reminder of her exceptional personality.'[51] The study collection no longer exists in its old form, in which the frames were not protected by glass, but Johanna van Nierop's memory is kept green by her many gifts to the museum and the copious notes, now in the textiles section, which she left behind on her documentary research.

The late thirties and the war years

Despite the economic problems of the thirties and the growing threat of war, Het Kantsalet saw its membership rise to 115 between 1937 and 1939. In 1938 an exhibition was held in the Museum Boymans in Rotterdam[52] and that same year saw the publication in collaboration with Het Kantsalet of Mien van der Meulen's book on lace.[53] Handsome gifts were also made to the Rijksmuseum in those years (cat. nos. 25, 37, 39). They even included a second flounce of *point de France* for an alb, a complete one this time (cat. no. 26).

From 25 August 1939, however, the collections of the Rijksmuseum were packed up and transported to places of safety for the duration of the war. The packing lists[54] clearly show that 19th-century pieces had formed part of the display, as was also the case in the study collection. Despite the difficulties of the Occupation, Het Kantsalet managed to keep going throughout the war years and even to present some further gifts of lace.

A new beginning

In 1946, problems of the Reconstruction notwithstanding, Het Kantsalet, which had long had a branch in Rotterdam and was now gradually to expand into a national organization, inaugurated the post-war era by presenting the Rijksmuseum with the splendid Argentan needle lace flounce with Chinoiserie figures (cat. no. 36), which one of its members, Mrs C. Visser-Wertheim, had acquired in Paris before the war. Three more fine pieces from her collection presented at the same time were a flounce from an alb of the type of bobbin lace in the Brussels technique generally known as

49 *Jaarverslag 1929*, p.12.
50 Archief van het Rijksmuseum, inv. 1499, no. 11623, minute of 20 December 1937.
51 *Jaarverslag 1938*, p. 20. In the United States Johanna van Nierop applied her talents to the lace collection in the Smithsonian Institution's National Museum of American History in Washington, D.C. I owe this information to Doris Bowman of that museum, who knew Miss van Nierop in her own early days there.
52 *Oude Kant 1938*.
53 Meulen-Nulle 1938; an English edition, *Lace*, published in 1963.
54 Archief van het Rijksmuseum, no. 2154.

fig. 5 Photograph of Kantsalet committee members made in Rotterdam in 1958, from left to right: Nellie Hudig, Mrs van Ras (treasurer), Anna Jiskoot-Pierson, Mrs A. Pierson-Muysken, Mien van der Meulen-Nulle. Archives of Het Kantsalet

Brabant lace, a border of Milanese lace (cat. no. 18) and a pair of Brussels needle lace lappets of the 1720s.[55]

1946 also saw the arrival in the Rijksmuseum of Miss A.M. Louise E. Erkelens (1915-1984) as assistant in charge of the textiles collection. She had not only a truly passionate love of lace, but also great powers of persuasion as far as the decision-makers in the museum were concerned, and so began what was to prove the most prosperous era in the history of the lace collection.

The remaining years of the forties were somewhat subdued as far as Kantsalet gifts were concerned, but in the fifties the society got back into its stride again. In 1950 it celebrated its silver jubilee with a special meeting at the Prinsenhof in Delft and the following year presented the Rijksmuseum with some pieces of Venetian needle lace bought with money contributed by members to mark the occasion (cat. no. 22). This was followed in 1953 and 1954 by yet more Italian cutwork (cat. no. 1) and lace (cat. no. 3). A sharp eye was now kept on auction sales, no doubt under the prompting of Louise Erkelens, lace being bought in 1954 from the sale of the Schouten Collection in Delft and 1955 from a sale at the Frederik Muller auction house in Amsterdam (cat. no. 34).

Het Kantsalet was, however, faced with something of a dilemma in that whereas 19th-century and even 20th-century lace had been acceptable in the past, Louise Erkelens was now generally rather reluctant to take pieces from Het Kantsalet that went beyond the Rijksmuseum's end date for collecting of c. 1830, although she occasionally accepted them from other sources. This meant that a fine and expensive piece of late 19th-century *point d'Angleterre* was given to the Museum Boijmans Van Beuningen in Rotterdam in 1951[56] and a Chantilly lace coiffure and a Brussels application lace scarf to the Nederlands Kostuummuseum (Netherlands Costume Museum) in The Hague in 1953. From this time onwards, therefore, Het Kantsalet no longer confined its generosity to the Rijksmuseum.

Gifts from elsewhere came in sporadically, notably two parasols donated by Johanna van Nierop and her sister from Washington D.C. in 1948 and 1950 and a selection, probably of family lace, from Baroness C.O. van Lynden in 1951. From the mid-fifties, however the museum increasingly began to purchase lace on its own account, especially after funds from the Commissie voor Fotoverkoop (Commission for Photograph Sales) became available later in the decade. The most spectacular purchase from the latter source came in 1958, when a Mr Z. Falkowski from Chicago turned up at the museum on 15 September with what was later described as a 'magnificent collection' of lace.[57] Numerous items were bought with Commission money (cat. nos. 42, 46) and a fine piece of Venetian raised needle lace, bought for the museum by Het Kantsalet (cat. no. 15) was, like so many pieces before it, given over for washing to 'the one woman in our country who is able to restore laces', namely Mien van der Meulen.[58]

Lace on display

In many of the displays arranged by Louise Erkelens, lace was shown in company with jewellery, small costume accessories and suchlike. This was true both of the first display arranged in 1952 (fig. 6) and a second of 1957 (fig. 7). A more permanent record of some of the pieces in the collection was also made available in *Kant* one of the picture books in the museum's 'Facetten der Verzameling' series,[59] in which over half the pieces illustrated were Kantsalet gifts and the lace was alternated with portraits showing comparable pieces.

In 1965 all the lace given by Het Kantsalet was exhibited to mark the society's 40th anniversary (fig. 8) and a catalogue was published.[60] In his introduction the then

55 Erkelens 1965, cat. no. 24, there called *Venise à reseau* (see no. 37).

56 Erkelens 1965, cat. no. 63 (as mid-19th century).
57 Archief van het Rijksmuseum, Textiel Correspondentie 1949-1959, letter of 15 December 1958.
58 Ibid. letter of 4 February 1959.
59 Erkelens 1955.
60 Erkelens 1965.

fig. 7 One of the showcases in the exhibition, 1957-1958

director of the Rijksmuseum, Arthur F.E. van Schendel (1910-1979), wrote, 'This society has always been so closely linked to the great national art collection that it is virtually self-evident that the birthday party should be given in its building.' He also pointed out that at long last the new display of the lace collection was nearing completion. This was to be found in the gallery adjacent to the costume display (fig. 9). The gifts made to the Rijksmuseum on this occasion (cat. nos. 30, 55) at last included a relatively large number of 19th-century pieces. This part of the collection was, however, shortly to be expanded in a spectacular manner.

Royal lace

In 1966 Queen Juliana of the Netherlands placed the major part of the royal lace collection on loan in the Rijksmuseum.[61] This brought the museum not only some fine examples of 17th and 18th-century lace (cat. nos. 14, 44), but, and perhaps even more importantly, a magnificent array of 19th-century lace (cat. nos. 51, 52, 53, 56-58, 63), not least pieces given to or acquired by Queen Emma after her arrival in the Netherlands in 1879 (cat. nos. 64, 65-69). Moreover, it was in this way that there came to the museum two characteristic pieces of Art Nouveau lace (cat. nos. 72, 75). Without the stim-

fig. 6 One of the showcases in the lace display of 1957-1958

61 Erkelens & Burgers 1966. For seven pieces on loan to the Centraal Museum, Utrecht, see Adriaans 1992-1993 and Wardle 1998.

fig. 8 General view of the exhibition marking the 40th anniversary of Het Kantsalet, 1965

fig. 9 View of part of the lace display in the 1960s.

fig. 10. View of part of the exhibition of the royal lace collection in the rooms of the Rijksprentenkabinet, 1966

ulus given to the Rijksmuseum's lace collection by Het Kantsalet, which had not only enriched the holdings, but also created the atmosphere in which donations had become the norm, it is unlikely that the royal loan would have been forthcoming. The exhibition of it mounted in 1966 in the rooms of the Rijksprentenkabinet came as a revelation to visitors (fig. 10).

Acquisitions in the sixties and seventies

It is highly ironic that while the Rijksmuseum had missed the turn of the century collecting boom altogether, it enjoyed one of its most active acquisition periods at a moment when the lace market was virtually defunct. By 1960 all the auction houses in London, for example, had ceased to sell lace, as there was no demand and it was not profitable any more. Only the Rijksmuseum and the Musées Royaux d'Art et d'Histoire in Brussels were still prepared to pay large sums for it. 1965 saw the first visit to the Rijksmuseum of the Paris art-dealer Madame L. Collette-Payre, on which occasion a flounce of *point de gaze* of the 1860s was acquired. Later acquisitions up to 1978 included fine examples of 17th

fig. 11 One of the showcases in the exhibition of the Jiskoot-Pierson Collection, 1970

and 18th-century lace (cat. nos. 12, 24, 31, 47), as well as some outstanding 19th-century work (cat. nos. 54, 60, 61). Het Kantsalet naturally kept up its annual gifts, most notably on its golden jubilee in 1975, when it presented almost sixty pieces (cat. nos. 2, 41, 47). It also became a tradition for members of the society or their heirs to leave or present lace to the museum on their deaths. In this way in 1970 the lace collection of a past president, Mrs Anna Jiskoot-Pierson (1891-1969), totalling over 200 pieces, was donated to the museum by her children (cat. nos. 35, 49) and made the subject of an exhibition (fig. 11)[62] and two years later lace collected by

her sister-in-law, Mrs A. Pierson-Muysken, also a past president, was given by her heirs (cat. nos. 13, 59).

In 1978 the superb gift of costumes made by Jonkvrouw C.I. Six included 17th-century lace cuffs long in the family's possession (cat. no. 10), as well as some fine lace-trimmed collars of the 1630s (cat. no. 9) and a whole collection of lace from the Teding van Berkhout family,

62 Erkelens 1970.

which had come to her from her uncle, the landscape-painter S.C. Bosch Reitz (1860-1930). This last was a typical family assemblage of lace, with the pieces mounted on and swathed in blue paper and stored in a tin trunk.[63] Louise Erkelens, now Mrs Mulder-Erkelens, retired in 1980. With her departure the days of large-scale lace collecting in the Rijksmuseum came to an end.

The period since 1980

The next textiles curator, C.A. Burgers, was still able to acquire some fine pieces from time to time: a magnificent *point de France* flounce (cat. no. 20) and other interesting items from the sale in London of the collection of Mrs Walter Burns in 1980 and the loan of a superb bobbin lace collar of the 1630s (cat. no. 11) the following year. A notable gift during his time was that of lace from

Mr and Mrs Van Haersma Buma-Six (cat. nos. 16, 62), including pieces bought by her grandfather in the 1890s. Burgers also mounted exhibitions, such as *40 years of lace* which illustrated collecting since the war years (fig.12), one of lace often seen in 17th-century portraits in 1984, one of 17th-century collars and later copies and imitations in 1985 and one of textiles from Twickel and Weldam, including lace, in 1991 (fig. 13). In 1980 he also invited the present author to work on the lace collection and since then it has been completely checked and reinventoried where necessary.

Under his successor, Mrs Ebeltje Hartkamp-Jonxis, presentations of lace have included fichus and shawls and displays relating to lace in the Netherlands in the 17th and 18th centuries,[64] while in the new gallery devoted to textiles and costume in the South Wing lace has figured in a number of presentations. Gifts of lace have continued to be made at intervals, but the collection has

63 Coppens 1995(2).

fig. 12 General view of part of the exhibition *40 years of lace*, 1987

64 Wardle 1992, 1994.

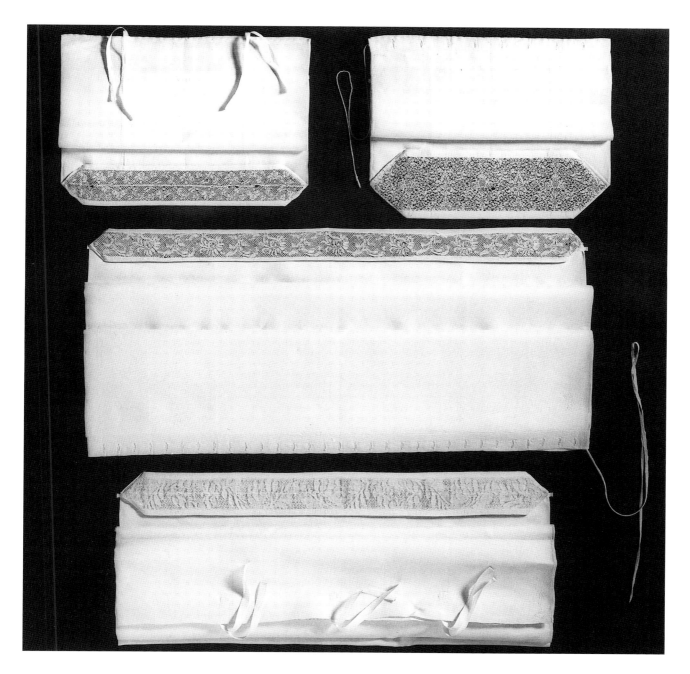

fig. 13 One of the showcases in the exhibition of pieces from Twickel and Weldam, 1991

almost ceased to grow by now.

Almost, but not quite, as Het Kantsalet is again making a splendid gesture to celebrate its 75th anniversary. This time it is presenting the Rijksmuseum with pieces from opposite ends of the lace spectrum: a showy dress of the early years of the 20th century (cat. no. 71) in a typical tape lace technique of that era, and a rare and fine ex-

ample of Spanish polychrome silk and gold and silver thread lace of the early 17th century (cat. no. 7), which is represented only in a very few collections either inside or outside Spain. Thus this latest gesture is yet another example of the continuing munificence without which the Rijksmuseum's lace collection would never have acquired the eminent position it enjoys today.

Catalogue

1

BORDER, CUT-WORK EMBROIDERY IN WHITE LINEN THREAD ON
LINEN IN BUTTONHOLE, SATIN AND STEM STITCHES AND BARS
AND NEEDLE LACE FILLINGS, EDGED BELOW WITH MACRAMÉ,
ITALY, C. 1600

---

226 x 18 cm
Inv. no. BK-1954-58
Provenance: collection of Alfred Lescure; purchased from art-dealer Mlle du Sartay,
Paris, 1954; donated by Het Kantsalet, 1954
Literature/Exhibition: Cox 1908, p. 21, fig. 11; Erkelens 1955, fig. 1; Erkelens 1965,
cat. no. 1; Burgers 1990(2), cat. no. 14; Lunghi & Pessa 1996, fig. 3

Cut-work embroidery, the basis from which needle lace
developed, began around the middle of the 16th century
with geometrical patterns governed by the threads of
the linen on which it was worked. Towards the middle
of the century in Italy much freer and more elaborate
designs came in under the influence of pattern books
such as those of Cesare Vecellio (c. 1521-1610) in Venice,
which ran into many editions between 1590 and 1625
(see cat. no. 3), and those of Isabella (Isabetta or Elisabetta) Catanea Parasole (active 1595-1625) published in
Rome between 1595 and 1636 (see cat. no. 2). The narrow
borders here still retain the old geometrical character,
but the main design is a bold symmetrical arrangement
of scrolling stems with large pomegranates and six-
petalled flowers, palmettes and hearts incorporating
leaves. Italian cut-work of this type sometimes also
includes small figures or hunting scenes.[1]

Along its lower edge the cut-work has a border of
macramé, a knotting technique of which the name is
thought to be derived from the Turkish *maqrama*, meaning towel or napkin, or the Arabic *miqramah*, meaning
striped cloth. The technique is thought to have been
introduced into Genoa and the surrounding area via
contacts with the Turks, a document of 1584 showing
that the term had already been in use there for some

time at that point.[2] Macramé was applied initially to the
valued objects decorated by the technique, such as the
long towels or covers that feature prominently in the
paintings of the Genoese artist Bernardo Strozzi (1581-
1644).[3] All the examples in Strozzi's paintings are finish-
es of warp threads, but macramé can also be worked
separately on a pillow, as must have been the case with
the border here. Macramé was one of the techniques that
enjoyed a revival at the end of the 19th century.

1. Gächter-Weber 1997, cat. no. 29; Davanzo Poli 1998, pp. 48-50.
2. Lunghi & Pessa 1996, Appendix.
3. Ibid., pp. 105-115.

2

BORDER, NEEDLE LACE, RETICELLA AND PUNTO IN ARIA,
SOUTHERN NETHERLANDS, 1600-1620

---

175 x 7 cm
Inv. no. BK-1975-366
Provenance: collection of Princesse Stéphanie Cantacuzène, Paris; donated by Het
Kantsalet on its golden jubilee, 1975
Literature/Exhibition: Burgers 1990(2), cat. no. 15

The fineness of the thread in this very delicate lace indicates that it must have been made in the Southern
Netherlands. Geometrical cut-work of an equally refined character appears on surviving caps of the second
half of the 16th century made there. The records of the
lace firm in Antwerp run by Martine Plantin (1550-1616)
and her sister Catherine (1553-1622), daughters of the
famous printer Christopher Plantin (1515-1589), show
them having cut-work made by workers not only in
Antwerp, but also as far afield as Mechelen, Brussels and
Breda.[1] It was only a short step from cut-work done on a
linen foundation to *reticella*, needle lace worked over a
grid of threads left in a piece of linen after the remaining
threads had been withdrawn, and *punto in aria*, needle

lace worked simply on a foundation of laid threads.

This *reticella* still retains the geometrical character which characterized the earliest work in the genre, but the *punto in aria* is more open and airy with little coils with bars and spots at intervals. These are reminiscent of those in some of the designs by Isabella Catanea Parasole, the wife of the woodcarver and printmaker Leonardo Parasole (c. 1570-c. 1630). She designed and made the woodcuts for no fewer than six pattern books between 1595 and 1615, some of which were reprinted as late as 1636. They contain not only fine geometric cutwork patterns, but also innovative designs with greater movement and variety, while the names of the techniques also appear over the designs.[2]

1. Risselin-Steenebrugen 1961, pp. 83, 91-92.
2. Graze, London/Chicago 1997, pp. 1068-1070.

3
BORDER, NEEDLE LACE, RETICELLA, WITH AN EDGING OF BOBBIN LACE, ITALY, 1600-1620

---

222 x 11 cm
Inv. no. BK-1953-46-A
Provenance: collection of Baroness De Constant Rebecque; collection of Gravin Dumonceau-De Constant Rebecque; donated by Het Kantsalet, 1953
Literature/Exhibition: Naber 1903, pl. 1, fig. 4; Oud-Italiaansche Kunst 1934, cat. no. 1187; Oude Kant 1938, cat. no. 116; Erkelens 1965, cat. no. 6; Burgers 1990(2), cat. no. 17

This *reticella* border is no longer worked on the threads of a piece of linen, but on a foundation of plaited threads laid over a parchment pattern. It consists of repeating patterns arranged alternately pointing to top left and bottom right. The design is one of the curious asymmetrical patterns in which a different motif appears on either side of a diagonal dividing the basic square of the *reticella* into two triangles. Designs of this type are only sparsely found in the pattern books. There is one, for

example, on fol. *6 of Corona delle nobile et virtuose donne, Libro primo* published in Venice in 1601,[1] which is by the painter and ornament designer Cesare Vecellio. Another example, which is more like the design of this lace, is found on fol. 24 of Isabella Catanea Parasole's *Teatro delle Nobile et Virtuose donne*, published in Rome in 1616.[2] Designs for small squares like those in the borders here are also found in Vecellio's books, as well as in in *Nuova Inventione* by Giacomo Franco (1550-1620), published in Venice in 1596,[3] and *Ghirlanda* by the printer and bookseller Pietro Paulo Tozzi (active 1596-1625), first published in Padua in 1604, which is a sort of compendium of female education, as it also includes calligraphy models, mathematical instruction, wise maxims and embroidery designs.[4] The narrow bobbin lace edging is a simple plaited lace of a type which goes back to the anonymous pattern book *Le Pompe*, first published in Venice in 1557.[5]

1. Lotz 1933, nos. 116-118.
2. Ibid., no. 143b.
3. Ibid. no. 131.
4. Ibid. no. 139c.
5. Lotz, nos. 95a-d and 100 a,b; Levey & Payne 1983.

4

BORDER, NEEDLE LACE, PROBABLY ITALY, 1600-1620

83 x 18 cm
Inv. no. BK-14858
*Provenance: collection of Leopold Iklé; collection of Fritz Iklé; possibly purchased direct
from the latter's sale Zürich, 28 December 1936; donated by Het Kantsalet, 1936
Literature/Exhibition: Iklé & Fäh n.d., pl. 5; Henneberg 1930, pl. 4; Erkelens 1965,
cat. no. 8; Levey 1983, pl. 67*

Although this striking lace, which must have been meant for furnishing purposes, was built up on a framework of plaited threads on a parchment pattern, it still preserves an aspect of *reticella* in the geometrical borders and also in the way stitches have been worked between the insertion and the border to suggest hem-stitching on linen.[1] The design with the large bird and leaves is difficult to relate to any of the pattern books.

A cloth in the Iklé Collection in the Textile Museum at St. Gallen in Switzerland, which is trimmed with needle lace with intertwined stems bearing semi-realistic flowers, including carnations, and heraldic crowned eagles with wings outstretched,[2] represents another stage in the development towards the Venetian needle lace with coiling stems and flowers (cat. no. 14).

1. Levey 1983, p. 14.
2. Iklé & Fäh n.d., no. 695.

5

SHEET, LINEN WITH DRAWN-THREAD WORK IN WHITE LINEN THREAD AND BOBBIN LACE, NORTHERN NETHERLANDS, PROBABLY FRIESLAND, C. 1600-1620

255 x 200 cm
Inv. no. BK-NM-2909
*Provenance: donated to the Nederlandsch Museum van Geschiedenis en Kunst by
Mr Eelco Verwys, 1876
Literature/Exhibition: Catalogus Leeuwarden 1922, p. 22, no.4; Van der Meulen-Nulle
1936, fig. 15*

The sheet bears the arms of the Van Dekema family and may have been made for Dr Sicke van Dekema (1548-1625), Lord of Tammenaburg at Hornhuizen in De Marne and owner of Mammemastate in Friesland, who was a member of the States of Friesland. The initials T for Tammenaburg and D for Dekema flank the arms.

The double line of hem-stitching and the extremely fine drawn-thread work of the arms, the letters and the borders patterned with hares and trees offer eloquent proof of the skills of Dutch and Frisian seamstresses in the 17th century. By 1600 exquisite needlework on the finest of linen already had a long tradition in the Low Countries. Martine and Catherine Plantin (see also cat. no. 2) were already selling collars and cuffs ornamented in this way in Antwerp in the mid-1540s.[1] In the Northern Netherlands bed linen continued to be decorated with needlework and cut-work for much of the 17th century, while linen was often marked with letters and numbers

done in the minutest of eyelet holes, again over counted threads.

The sheet further has borders and insertions of plaited bobbin lace in a pattern imitating the geometrical designs of contemporary *reticella* and *punto in aria* and of a type which also goes back to the mid-16th century and appears originally to have been denoted by the term 'brainat' (in various spellings) in the Low Countries.[2] It was made in the Northern as well as the Southern Netherlands in the 17th century: 'beautiful handwork and Breynaet' are listed in the last book of calligraphy models published by Maria Strick (1577-after 1631) in 1618 as being among the accomplishments taught in the French schools that she and her husband ran in Delft and Rotterdam.[3] Surviving documentation on lacemaking in Friesland is sparse, but in the 1622 inventory of Antie Wilhelmi, wife of the Leeuwarden linen merchant Corst Reneman, mention is made of three lace-makers, all with Frisian names, which suggests that the craft was quite well established there by that time.[4] Thus this fine sheet might possibly have been entirely local work.

1. Risselin-Steenebrugen 1961, p. 83.
2. Ibid., pp. 86-87.
3. The list of accomplishments comes in the sonnet by Guillaume Sylvius in *De Schat oft Voorbeeldt ende Verthooning van Verscheyden Beschriften...Door Maria Strick*. For Maria Strick's life see Haverkorn van Rijsewijk 1905.
4. Henstra 1992, p. 76.

6

COVER, LACIS AND BOBBIN LACE, WITH THE ARMS OF SICKINGHE AND JONGEMA, THE INITIALS OVS AND THE DATE 1623, NORTHERN NETHERLANDS, FRIESLAND, 1623

110 x 110 cm
Inv. no. BK-KOG-9
Provenance: collection of Nicolaas Pieneman; bequeathed to the Koninklijk Oudheidkundig Genootschap, 1860; on loan from the Koninklijk Oudheidkundig Genootschap
Literature/Exhibition: Van der Meulen-Nulle 1952, 1963, fig. 3; Levey 1983, fig. 94; Burgers 1990(1), pp. 56-57, figs. 12, 13; Wardle 1992(2), fig. 4

The initials OVS are those of Oedt van Sickinghe, the daughter of Johan Sickinghe (d. 1652) and Luts Laesd. van Jongema, who married Poppe Bockes van Sickinghe in 1634.[1] It may be that she learnt to make *lacis* as one of the forms of needlework taught at school, so that she could have made this cloth herself. Many of the motifs come from a favourite source of the time, namely the pattern books of Johannes Sibmacher (d. 1611), the Nüremberg painter and engraver. The vase flanked by lions and oak sprigs is from his *Schön Neues Modelbuch* of

6a. Lion rampant and other motifs from Johann Sibmacher, *Schön Neves Modelbuch*, 1597. Det Danske Kunstindustrimuseum, Copenhagen

1597 (fig. 6a), the corner motifs from his *Newes Modelbuch in Kupfer gemacht* of 1601, which was reprinted in 1604.[2] It was one of the most popular pattern books ever produced. Motifs from it were used in embroidery well into the 18th century, while the facsimiles published in 1874 and 1886[3] brought the designs back into favour again.[4] The popularity of Sibmacher's designs in the Dutch Republic is evinced not only by the appearance of motifs in samplers,[5] but also by the existence at Kasteel Twickel of another *lacis* cover, even finer than this one and of about the same period, which features the lion and vase motif again, along with a peacock pattern, and was probably made in the province of Gelderland, since it bears in the corners the quarterings of the arms of Catharina van Arnhem (1574-1639).[6] Like Oedt van Sickinghe's cover that of Catharina van Arnhem has a border of plaited bobbin lace, which might possibly also have been made in the Northern Netherlands (see cat. no. 5).

Both covers were probably table or cupboard cloths. The 1632 inventory of the Stadholder's Quarter and his house at Noordeinde in The Hague lists cupboard cloths of *lacis* as well as summer bed hangings in the technique.[7]

1. Burgers 1990(1), note 43.
2. Ibid, note 44; Burgers in Luijten et al 1993, cat. no. 169; Lotz 1933, nos. 32a, 38a; Jong & Groot 1988, no. 446; Paludan & Hemmer Egeberg 1991, nos. 35, 36, figs. 43, 44.
3. Paludan & Hemmer Egeberg 1991, no. 37.
4. Wardle 1969.
5. Cf. Schipper-van Lottum, figs. 170, 171 and elsewhere.
6. Burgers in Luijten et al 1993, cat. no. 169.
7. Ibid., note 5.

BORDER, SILK AND METAL THREAD NEEDLE LACE, SPAIN, 1615-1630

57 x 60.5 cm, width of lace 9.5 cm
Inv. no. BK-2000-3
Provenance: purchased from art-dealer Jonathan Page, Honiton, England; donated by Het Kantsalet to mark its 75th anniversary, 2000

This type of silk and metal thread lace is not well known outside Spain. It has received only sporadic mention in the lace literature, even though it is highly distinctive and unlike any other lace. The buttonhole stitching is worked in coloured silks over silver and silver-gilt threads, which gleam through the silk to create a sumptuous effect. This lace was much used for edging chalice veils and velvet covers for domestic use. It is called *frisado de Valladolid* in Spain, because a great deal of it was produced in convents there.[1]

The design of the Rijksmuseum border with its floral motifs, scrolls and slanting elements, is very typical not only of Spanish silk and metal lace of the 17th century, but also of contemporary Spanish embroidery in silk and metal thread on linen, which may also feature areas of cut-work spanned by metal threads. A number of designs of this type with the conspicuous slanting element are to be found in Isabella Parasole's *Teatro delle Nobilli et Virtuose Donne* published in Rome in 1616 (fig. 7a). This book is dedicated to the Spanish princess Dona Elisabetta Borbona, while an earlier pattern book by Parasole, *Studio delle virtuose Donne*, first published in Rome in 1597, is dedicated to the wife of the then Spanish ambassador, Dona Juana d'Aragon. However, it is not possible to tell whether the designs were inspired by Spanish models or whether they were actually used in Spain. They are labelled as being for 'ponto in aria', but

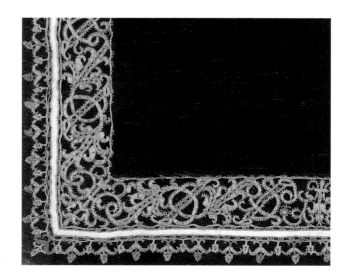

7a. Design from Isabella Parasole, *Teatro delle Nobilli et Virtuose Donne*, Rome 1616, fol.9

they could have lent themselves equally well to the silk and metal thread lace and to embroidery.

Later in the 17th century this lace, like Venetian lace (cat. no. 11), developed freer designs with trailing stems of often recognizable flowers, such as borage, tulip, carnation and columbine, and a ground of bars or even mesh. A notable example of this later work is a large cover in the Österreichisches Museum für Angewandte Kunst in Vienna, which is said to have come from the Hapsburg collections.[2]

1. Davanzo Poli 1984, p. 307.
2. Schuette 1963, pl. 32; see also Iklé & Fäh, n.d., pl. 10, bottom, and Besselièvre 1913, pl. 39.

8
BORDER, BOBBIN LACE, ITALY, GENOA, OR SOUTHERN NETHERLANDS, 1620-1630

410 x 13 cm
Inv. no. BK-1953-49
Provenance: collection of Baroness de Constant Rebecque; collection of Gravin du Monceau-de Constant Rebecque; donated by Het Kantsalet, 1953
Literature/Exhibition: Naber 1903, pl. XI. fig.1; Erkelens 1955, fig. 6; Erkelens 1965, cat. no. 36; Burgers 1990(2), cat. no. 24

The influence of the geometrical patterns of *reticella* can still be seen in this bobbin lace, which predates the development of more elaborate designs later in the 17th century. The presence of wheat-ear motifs suggests an Italian origin, as they are generally held to be characteristic of the bobbin lace that has traditionally come to be associated with Genoa. However, heavier bobbin lace very similar to this also began to be made in Flanders around 1620, so the precise attribution remains an open question. The deep scallops are characteristic of the 1620s, as is the design with two motifs in the centre surrounded by a scalloped border.[1] Lace like this appears on collars and cuffs in many Dutch and Flemish portraits of the period (fig. 8a).

Around 1900, when there was a revival of old lace techniques of all kinds, this type of lace was much imitated, notably by the lace firm established by Mario Zennaro (1881-1962) at Rapallo in Liguria in 1908.[2] Creditable imitations were also produced by the lace school run by the Ursuline nuns of Fagagna near Gorizia in Friuli.[3] These imitations do have a certain rigidity and lifelessness about them, however.

1. Cf. Risselin-Steenebrugen 1980, fig. 231, Coppens 1981, cat. no. 3, Levey 1983, fig. 113.
2. Parma Armani 1990, pp. 70, 99.
3. Davanzo Poli 1984, p. 96.

8a. Nicolaes Eliasz. called Pickenoy, *Maria Joachimsdr Swartenhout* (1598-1631), dated 1627. Inv. no. A 699

9a. Wybrand Symonsz de Geest (1592-after 1660), *Prince Willem Frederik of Nassau-Dietz* (1613-1664), signed and dated 1632. Inv. no. A 530

9

FALLING COLLAR, LINEN WITH NEEDLE LACE, RETICELLA AND PUNTO IN ARIA, MARKED h2, COLLAR: NORTHERN NETHERLANDS, LACE: PROBABLY ITALY 1625-1640

W. of collar 66 cm, of lace 16 cm
Inv. no. BK-1978-462
Provenance: donated by Jonkvrouw C.I. Six, 1978
Literature/Exhibition: Burgers 1990(2) cat. no. 10; Bruggeman 1997, p. 43

This collar and another, also with needle lace, came to the Rijksmuseum with the Six gift, but it is not clear whether they were old family possessions or bought around the turn of the century by Professor J. Six (1857-1926) for his collection. In either case, however, the collar as such was very probably made in the Northern Netherlands. The needle lace, which still has a geometrical design, is most probably from Italy, of some very similar borders in the Como municipal collections.[1] A well-known engraving of c. 1637 by Abraham Bosse (1602-1676) of a row of shops in the Galerie du Palais (Royal) in Paris shows the boutique of a *mercier* or mercer with lace-trimmed falling collars and cuffs hung up at

was much favoured for wear at masquerades. There was also a fashion for having one's portrait painted in 17th-century attire, which extended to some artists who no doubt wished thereby to gain some of the allure of illustrious predecessors. These developments are represented in the Rijksmuseum by two much later examples. In a signed and dated self portrait of 1874 the history painter Hendrik Hollander Cz (1823-1884), who was a pupil of Nicolaas Pieneman (1809-1860) and like him acquired a collection of art objects, is attired in a Rembrandtesque costume, complete with lace collar (fig 9b), while a set of collar and cuffs trimmed with bobbin lace made in imitation of 17th-century lace was made at the Koninklijke Nederlandsche Kantwerkschool in The Hague for a participant in the students' pageant of 1910 at Leiden University.[3]

1. Rizzini 1996, nos 10, 11.
2. Dillon 1929-1974, Vol. III, no. 666.
3. Inv. nos BK-1975-372-a,b,c. Wardle 1992(1), cat. no. 40.

9b. Hendrik Hollander Cz (1823-1884), *Self Portrait*, signed and dated 1876. Inv. no. A 1489

the back, while lace-trimmed fichus are draped over the counter. This boutique is next to one selling gloves. In Amsterdam the two commodities were found in combination in the shop of the widow of Daniel Guiot on Warmoesstraat, where separate inventories were drawn up in 1642 of the gloves and the linen and lace, which included lace-trimmed collars, shirts, handkerchiefs and men's nightcaps.[2] Lace-trimmed falling collars enjoyed a revival in many parts of Europe towards the middle of the 18th century, when 17th-century costume

10

CUFF, LINEN WITH BOBBIN LACE, CUFF: NORTHERN NETHERLANDS, LACE: SOUTHERN NETHERLANDS, 1630-1640

39 x 14 cm
Inv. no. BK-1978-464
Provenance: Six family; donated by Jonkvrouw C.I. Six, 1978
Literature/Exhibition: Six 1932, p. 9, fig. 7; Burgers 1990(2), cat. no. 12;
Wardle 1995, pp. 62-63

This cuff is the finest of those in the possession of the Six family, which were published by Professor J. Six in 1932. He suggested that the lace might have been made in the

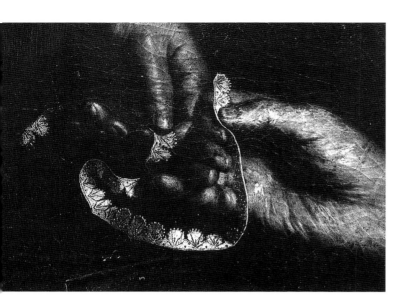

10a. Detail from Dirck Dircksz. Santvoort (1610-1680). *The Regentesses of the House of Correction, Amsterdam, 1638.* City of Amsterdam, on loan to the Amsterdams Historisch Museum.

Northern Netherlands, but while that could perhaps apply to some of the lace on the other two pairs of cuffs,[1] that on this example is of a fineness which must indicate that it was made in the Southern Netherlands. The wide border of lace has the vase of flowers motif, which was dominant in Flemish bobbin lace in the 1630s and which derives ultimately from the pattern books by Bartolomeo Danieli (see cat. no. 11). The lace is a 'part lace', which means that the motifs were made separately first and then joined together. This technique had already come into being by the end of the 16th century and was later to be associated exclusively with Brussels lace.[2] The fine linen thread available to the Flemish lace-makers enabled them to produce a supple, but often elaborately patterned lace, which was ideally suited to the new falling collars that gradually came into fashion in the early decades of the 17th century.

Lace of this type long remained popular in the Dutch Republic, where it appears in portraits from the 1620s to the 1640s. Some of the simpler forms of bobbin lace were, indeed, made in the Republic. In a group portrait of 1638 by Dirck Dircksz Santvoort (1610-1680) of *The Regentesses of the House of Correction* in Amsterdam (fig. 10a) the regentess Lijsbert Hendricksdr Haecken is being handed a piece of lace for inspection

by one of the 'house-mothers', the inference obviously being that lace making was one of the activities engaged in by the inmates. Records too reveal that much lace was made by women and girls in similar institutions and orphanages as well as by linen seamstresses and others.[3]

1. One of these pairs also came to the Rijksmuseum, inv. no. BK-1978-463-a,b.
2. Levey 1983, pp. 22-23.
3. Wardle 1983, pp. 8-10.

11

FALLING COLLAR, LINEN WITH BOBBIN LACE, MARKED IW FOR ADMIRAL JACOB VAN WASSENAER VAN KERNHEIM EN OBDAM (1610-1665), COLLAR: NORTHERN NETHERLANDS, LACE: SOUTHERN NETHERLANDS, 1630-1640,

---

50 x 79 cm
Inv. no. BK-BR-934
Provenance: passed down in the Van Wassenaer Obdam family to Marie-Cornelie, Countess Van Wassenaer Obdam, who inherited the country house Twickel in 1812, and thence to the descendants of the daughter of her husband, J.D.C. Baron van Heekeren by his second marriage; on loan to the Rijksmuseum, 1981
Literature/Exhibition: Burgers 1992, cat. no. 9; Wardle 1992(2), fig. 1

Before this splendid collar was conserved in 1985 it had attached to it a note written in 1767 by the Dowager Countess Unico Wilhelm van Wassenaer Obdam (1702-1769) to the effect that it belonged to her husband's great-grandfather, Admiral Jacob van Wassenaer van Obdam (1547-1623). However, the style of the lace shows that it is much more likely to have been worn by the later Admiral Jacob van Wassenaer van Kernheim en Obdam (1610-1665). The collar has both a lace edging and a matching insertion, which makes it exceptionally rich. The design of the lace, with its pots of flowers and scrolling elements, resembles some of the patterns in *Vari disegni de merletti* by Bartolomeo Danieli, published in

11a. Rembrandt van Rijn (1606-1669), *Marten Soolmans* (1613-1641), signed and dated 1634. Private collection, Paris

365 x 43 cm
Inv. no. BK-1967-140
Provenance: purchased from art-dealer Madame L. Collette-Payre, Paris, 1967
Literature/Exhibition: Burgers 1990(2), cat. no. 20

The medallions in the border of this striking flounce still retain in their centres an echo of the geometrical *reticella* motifs of the early days of needle lace, but the exuberant coiling stems with tulips, tiger lilies and other flowers are characteristic of early baroque design in lace. Coiling stem patterns, which derive ultimately from Classical Antiquity, were much used for embroidery from at least the mid-16th to the mid-17th century. Patterns of this kind for needle lace were published in Siena as early as 1610 by Bartolomeo Danieli, who gave his profession as *recamatore* or embroiderer, under the title *Fiore pretioso d'orni vertu* and reprinted in Bologna around 1630 as *Libro di diversi disegni*. Borders here with coiling stems enclosing quite realistic flowers resemble those in the Rijksmuseum's lace,[1] while similar designs of a more asymmetrical type, reminiscent of the floral motifs between the medallions, are found in the last, untitled designs by Danieli, this time for bobbin lace, which were published in Bologna around 1643.[2]

Comparable flounces of very similar design featuring medallions amid coiling stems with flowers are to be

Bologna in 1639,[1] which was the last important lace pattern book to appear on the market. However, the fineness of the thread leaves no doubt that the lace was made in the Southern Netherlands. The lace of the insertion has the lower section of the motifs on the lobes arranged upwards and downwards alternately, whereas in a comparable collar in the Musée National de La Renaissance, Château d'Ecouen, in France the lobes and insertions feature different vase patterns.[2]

Admiral Jacob van Wassenaer van Kernheim en Obdam may have worn this collar for his wedding in 1633. A sumptuous collar of a similar design appears in the marriage portrait of 1634 by Rembrandt (1606-1669) of Marten Soolmans (1613-1641), a member of a wealthy Amsterdam family, who was also married in 1633 (fig.11a).

1. Lotz 1933, no. 149; Levey 1983, fig. 112.
2. Kraatz 1992, cat. no. 85.

seen on three albs of the same period in the Museo Diocesano in Venice[3] and there can be little doubt that this lace was made in Venice itself. It marks one of the later and most important stages in the transition from geometrical cut-work to the heavy raised Venetian lace of later in the century, which was to be used by the church for whole vestments.[4]

Naturally, lace like the Rijksmuseum flounce was also employed domestically and for costume. A portrait in the Uffizi Gallery in Florence, formerly identified as Charles Emanuel of Savoy, shows a magnificent falling collar of it with interlinked stems bearing exotic flowers.[5]

1. Lotz 1933, fig. 100: 197, see nos. 144 and 148b in the text.
2. Ibid., fig. 106: 208, 209, see no. 151 in the text.
3. Strinati; 1926, p. 35.
4. See, for example, a chasuble in the Victoria & Albert Museum, London, Trendell 1930, frontispiece.
5. Levey, 1953, fig. 134.

13
BORDER, BOBBIN LACE, SOUTHERN NETHERLANDS, 1645-1655

85 x 12.5 cm
Inv. no. BK-1973-71
Provenance: collection of Mrs A. Pierson-Muysken, former President of Het Kantsalet;
donated by her children, 1973

Towards the middle of the 17th century the scallops of Flemish bobbin lace borders became ever shallower,

until all that remained of them was a slightly wavy edge, as in this border. The designs also became denser. They could still sometimes incorporate the favourite motif of a pot of flowers, as here, but quite often there is no semblance of a pot any more and the design has become highly stylized. This border is a part lace, made in sections which are clearly visible, while the motifs are set against a ground worked round them after they were completed and showing the first beginnings of a mesh. Lace like this appears in many portraits around 1650

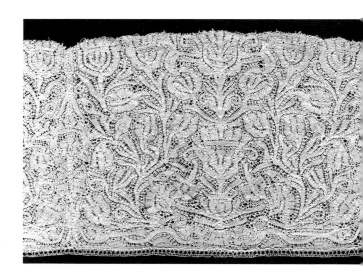

13a. Ferdinand Bol (1616-1780), *Maria Rey* (1630/31-1730), signed and dated 1650. Inv. no. A 684

14a. Hendrick Cornelisz. van (der) Vliet (1611/12-1675), *Portrait of a Woman Aged 27*, signed and dated 28 August 1663. Inv. no. A 1343

trimming the wide linen collars favoured at the time. These were now adorned with just a single border of lace, but women often achieved a rich effect nonetheless by layering a kerchief over a falling collar (fig. 13a)

This border, which is completely straight-edged, has a closely packed design of two alternating coiling stem motifs, one of a spreading type, the other compact. Each motif is symmetrical around a central axis of a row of flower forms. The motifs are outlined by rows of holes, while the ground shows the beginnings of a mesh.

This kind of lace was so popular in the Dutch Republic and appears in so many Dutch portraits that it came to be known in the 19th century as 'Dutch lace', but while some lace of this type might possibly have been produced in the Republic, most of it and certainly the best sort will have come from the Southern Netherlands. A portrait of 1663 shows how perfectly it lent itself to the wide

14
BORDER, BOBBIN LACE, SOUTHERN NETHERLANDS, 1650-1665

117 x 10 cm (in two pieces)
Inv. no. BK-BR-J-162
Provenance: probably inventory of Queen Emma, no. 131b, bought from Frenckel in Utrecht, 1913; a loan from the Koninklijke Verzamelingen, The Hague, 1966
Literature/Exhibition: Erkelens & Burgers 1966, cat. no. 160

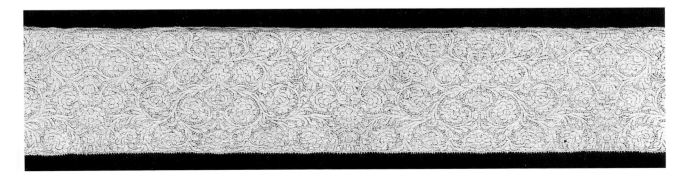

flat collars of the period and to cuffs which were only slightly gathered (fig. 14a). The flowers on the sitter's silk dress here are very similar to those on the lace and it is clear that other silks of the period with floral sprig patterns inspired the lace designers.[1]

The account book of Wendela Bicker (1635-1668), daughter of a wealthy Amsterdam Regent family, who married Grand Pensionary Johan de Witt (1625-1672) in 1655, reveals the large amounts that were spent on lace at this period.[2] In 1655 the couple owned lace to the value of 1,011 guilders, an enormous sum by comparison with the 6 guilders paid for the making of one of Wendela's gowns. That most of the lace was Flemish lace of a kind similar to this border is suggested by the portraits of the couple painted in 1659, in which Wendela is wearing a very wide flat collar and cuffs of it and Johan a collar bordered with it.[3] Perhaps Wendela's lace was the set 'bought when I was married', which cost a hefty 187 guilders and 10 stuivers.[4] In 1664, however, when she had the lace as a whole valued again, its worth, excluding a set of sleeve ruffles valued at 150 guilders bequeathed to her by her sister, had fallen to 300 guilders. This is perhaps not surprising, since it had virtually all been reused either on her own or her children's clothes. Even in a wealthy household like this thrift prevailed, which may help to explain why there are almost no examples in the Rijksmuseum's collection of the best quality lighter and more open Flemish bobbin laces, which developed later in the 17th century (see the collar and cuffs worn by Geertruida den Dubbelde, fig. 17a).

1. Levey 1983, fig. 151.
2. Kinderen-Besier 1950, Appendix II; Kuus 1997.
3. Kuus 1997, figs. 1,2.
4. Der Kinderen-Besier, p. 273.

15

FURNISHING BORDER, RAISED NEEDLE LACE, ITALY, VENICE, 1660-1675

200 x 28 cm
Inv. no. BK-1958-89
Provenance: collection of Z. Falkowski, Chicago; donated by Het Kantsalet, 1958
Literature/Exhibition: Erkelens 1965, cat. no. 10; Burgers 1990(2), cat. no. 34

This symmetrical design of scrolling stems with elaborate, convoluted leaves and flowers is characteristic of heavy raised Venetian lace, the superb baroque textile which rapidly became high fashion in Europe after the mid-17th century. Although now often denoted by the French term *gros point de Venise*, in Venice itself this lace was generally called *punto Venezia a relievi* or Venetian point with relief. The complex technique, with raised edges worked over bundles of threads and many filling patterns to give subtle nuances of light and shade, developed out of that of the earlier needle lace with coiling stem designs (see cat. no. 11). Now motifs were sometimes made separately, enabling large pieces to be produced.

The designs echo those of some of the Italian woven silks of the day, but little is known about the designers. However, the name of one of them is preserved on a partly worked parchment in the Venetian civic collection, which is inscribed *PAB. Piero Cupilli San Cassan Inv.*[1]. Apart from such rare survivals, there appears to be very little documentation on this extraordinarily successful industry. The earliest document discovered to date is an inventory of 1671 of the Venetian lace merchant Giovanni Francesco Vecellio, which shows that Venetian

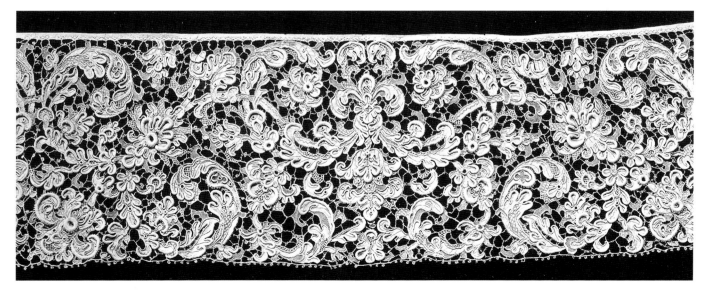

needle lace was far more expensive than the local bobbin lace and at least three times dearer than the best French and Flemish bobbin lace which the shop also sold.[2] In the same year Monsigneur de Bouzy, Bishop of Béziers, reported to Louis XIV's minister Colbert in France that 'All the convents of the religious and all the poor families live off this work here', the convent of San Zaccaria being the most famous for its fine lace.[3]

Heavy borders like this would have been used for furnishing. Several even wider borders from covers of velvet or other rich materials have survived, some of them from former royal collections.[4]

1. Davanzo Poli 1984, p. 25 left.
2. Kraatz 1984, p.131.
3. Lefébure 1887, p. 22.
4. Levey 1983, fig. 183; Paludan et al 1991, cat. no. 54.

16
COLLAR, RAISED NEEDLE LACE, ITALY, VENICE, 1660-1675

---

93 x 19 cm
Inv. no. BK-1991-8
Provenance: donated by Mr and Mrs Van Haersma Buma-Six, 1991
Literature/Exhibition: Wardle 1992(2), fig. 6

In the 1660s a new kind of collar with two wide panels in front came into vogue for men. The most fashionable and expensive examples were soon being made entirely of the new raised needle lace from Venice with striking designs like this one, in which each half of the collar is occupied by a single bold elongated scroll, the two together forming a symmetrical pattern. The effect of the scroll is softened by the many leaves and flowers and playful features such as unexpected loops and curls in the main stem. A similar, in places even more fanciful,

16b. Caspar Netscher (1639-1684), *Coenraad van Beuningen (1622-1693)*, signed and dated 1673. City of Amsterdam, on loan to the Amsterdams Historisch Museum. Inv. no. C 193

1674 for 'Three rich Poynts de Venise for three Bands [i.e. collars of this type] and Six Yards sutable for four paire of Cuffs' supplied by his 'laceman' John Eaton. These were by far the most expensive items in a large bill for lace, which amounted in all to over £777.[2]

1. Lefébure 1887, p.213.
2. Wardle 1997, p.21.

effect can be seen in a design for such a collar with scrolls of almost equal boldness centred on a formal motif in the middle of the back (fig. 16a). It must have been a collar like this that the then French ambassador to Venice, the Comte d'Avaux, sent to Colbert in January 1673, eliciting the comment, 'I have received in good order the needlepoint collar with relief work that you have sent me and which I think very beautiful'. He could not help adding, however, 'I compared it with those to be found in our manufactures, but I must tell you in advance that equally beautiful ones are made in this realm'.[1]

Among portraits in the Rijksmuseum showing collars of this rich lace is one of 1673 by Caspar Netscher (1639-1684) of Coenraad van Beuningen (1622-1693), burgo-master of Amsterdam, statesman and diplomat, whose status is further enhanced by his cuffs and shirt frill of equally costly Venetian lace (fig. 16b). The conspicuous consumption that this represented is clear from the sum of over £159 paid by Charles II of England (1660-1685) in

16a. Design for a bib-fronted band, Venice, 1660-1675, Cooper-Hewitt National Design Museum, New York

17

BORDER, BLACK SILK BOBBIN LACE, PROBABLY FRANCE, C. 1670

41 x 9 cm
Inv. no. BK-NM-VI-R
Provenance: unknown
Literature/Exhibition: Wardle 1985, pp. 220-222; Wardle 1992(2), fig. 7

17a. Bartholomeus van der Helst (1613-1670), *Geertruida den Dubbelde (1647-1684),* signed and dated 1668. Inv. no. A 141

This rare surviving example of 17th-century black silk lace is associated with, but not necessarily part of, the remains of a cap composed of black silk lace of two different patterns. The elegant design of two alternating symmetrical motifs is at once a more open and a more stylized version of that of Flemish bobbin lace of the previous decade, but while many of the motifs have a more formal character, the flowers can be seen as representations of tulips and roses. The motifs are bounded by a line of holes and the lace has a torchon ground. The best black silk lace of this type was made in the Paris area at this period in the 17th century,[1] but samples among the papers of the textile merchant Jacques de Lannoy in Antwerp suggest that it was also made in the Southern Netherlands.[2]

Although hardly any black silk lace survives, it was, of course, much used in the Dutch Republic in the 17th century. The rich black silk clothes of the wealthy regent class were often trimmed with laid on black lace of a rather heavy type in the earlier years. The lighter forms, such as the Rijksmuseum piece, which came in after the middle of the century, were used to edge women's gowns in such a way that their designs could clearly be seen over white sleeves or light-coloured petticoats (fig. 17a), while men often favoured a rich array of black and white sleeve ruffles.

1. Buffevant 1984.
2. Information kindly supplied by Frieda Sorber.

18

BORDER, MILANESE BOBBIN LACE, NORTHERN ITALY, 1675-1700

340 x 19 cm
Inv. no. BK-16005
Provenance: collection of Mrs C. Visser-Wertheim; purchased by Het Kantsalet from Mrs
M. Visser; donated by Het Kantsalet, 1946
Literature/Exhibition: Van der Meulen-Nulle 1959, fig. 40, 1963, fig. 42; Erkelens 1955,
fig. 15; Erkelens 1965, cat. no. 39; Burgers 1990(2), cat. no. 32

This type of baroque bobbin lace, in which there are relatively few or sometimes no bars joining the motifs is generally called Milanese, but it was probably made in many places in Northern Italy, Venice and Genoa among them.[1] The symmetrical design of this border is centred on an elaborate version of the flowering plant in a pot motif, dramatically flanked by two sets of curving leaves and various other leaves and flowers. The delineation is bold, but exhibits a certain clumsiness and the same is true of a large panel of the same type of lace in the Musée Historique des Tissus at Lyon, where comparable elements are to be seen.[2] The two pieces also evince the same rows of holes in the outlines of the motifs and the same variety of decorative fillings, but the Lyon piece has a mesh ground, the Rijksmuseum one bars. This type of lace was much favoured for church use, but the presence of hunting figures in the Lyon panel clearly indicates that it was used for secular purposes as well, its boldness making it an ideal furnishing lace. Variants of Milanese lace continued to be made well into the 18th century.

This and the similar lace made in the Southern Netherlands, which is distinguished by the fact that the threads of the ground are often carried over the pattern elements at the back of the work, enjoyed a revival in the 19th century. This is said to have begun in the late 1840s, when a Mlle Marie van Outryve d'Ydewalle made a careful study of a Flemish lace on an altar-cloth in Bruges and developed a version of the technique. The lace, made around Bruges, Iseghem and Thiele, received favourable notice at the Paris Exhibition of 1867, but it was in the decades around the turn of the century that it became a popular fashion lace, under the names of *guipure de Flandres* or *point de Milan*.[3]

1. Levey 1983, pp. 33-34.
2. Ibid., fig. 208; Kraatz 1983, cat. no. 44 (there ascribed to Spain).
3. Wardle 1968, pp. 126-127.

19

MAN'S COLLAR OR BIB-FRONTED BAND, SMALL-SCALE VENETIAN
NEEDLE LACE, ITALY, VENICE, 1675-1700

Each front: 24 x 17 cm
Inv. no. BK-1963-106
Provenance: on loan from Mrs E.H. Egidius-Van Doorninck, 1935; donated by her, 1963
Literature/Exhibition: Bruggeman 1997, p. 50 right

Venetian needle lace was not always of the heavy raised variety in the third decade of the 17th century, but the smaller scale form of it undoubtedly became more popular in the decades thereafter, which saw the rise to prominence of *point de France*. This collar has an unusually elegant pattern of scrolling branches in which the leaf forms predominate over the flowers and relatively minor use is made of filling patterns. The ground is of bars with picots.

The kind of establishment in which expensive lace like this was sold in the Dutch Republic is revealed by an advertisement of 9 February 1686 in the *Amsterdamse Courant* regarding the sale of the stock of the 'highly renowned and costly French Haberdasher's Shop' of the late Daniel Guiserit. This included 'all kinds of Point de Venise, France, La Reine, d'Espagne and English gold and silver lace', alongside watches, medallions, 'rareties in tortoiseshell, curiously painted fans' and other similar goods.[1] Venetian lace was so expensive that it is no surprise to learn that less costly versions or imitations of it were made. The term 'La Reine' seems to have been applied mainly in Northern Europe to a flat needle lace

of Venetian type,[2] 'Point d'Espagne' appears to have been a form of needle lace or possibly tape lace similar to, but cheaper than Venetian lace.[3] The same name was later used to denote gold lace, but in the late 17th and early 18th centuries that was generally referred to as 'point d'Espagne d'or'.[4]

1. From the notes of Johanna van Nierop in the Rijksmuseum.
2. Levey 1983, p. 40.
3. Wardle 1997, p. 21.
4. Levey 1983, pp. 38, 55.

20

FLOUNCE, NEEDLE LACE, POINT DE FRANCE, FRANCE, 1685-1695

---

335 x 65 cm
Inv. no. BK-1980-86
Provenance: collection of Mrs Walter Burns, née Mary Lyman Morgan, sister of J. Pierpont Morgan; collection of her daughter Lady Harcourt, née Mary Ethel Haynes Burns; inherited by her daughter the Hon. Mrs John Mulholland, née Olivia Vernon; purchased by the Rijksmuseum at sale London (Christie's), 26 February 1980, no. 122
Literature/Exhibiton: Burgers 1990(2), cat. no. 1; Wardle 1996, pp. 27-29

Lace of this design is now the most famous to have survived from the period when the needle lace known as *point de France* left its Venetian origins behind and

branched out on its own. The story began on 5 August 1665, when a government-sponsored lace industry was established in France by Louis XIV's minister Jean Baptiste Colbert (1619-1683) largely in order to compete with Venetian needle lace, the extensive importation of which was proving a great drain on the French economy.[1] Thirty lace factors and skilled workers were brought from Venice to Alençon in Normandy, which, with neighbouring Argentan, was to become the centre for French needle lace. Bobbin lace industries on the Flemish model were also set up at the same time and both types of lace were initially called *point de France*, but that name soon came to be applied to the needle lace alone.

At first the needle lace followed Venetian developments, but late in the 17th century there was a switch to French design, which at that time was dominated by Jean Bérain (1637-1711), who had been appointed *Dessinateur de la Chambre et du Cabinet du Roi* in 1674. The design of this lace is distinctly Bérainesque in style, with its theatrical figures, crowns, canopies, obelisks, trophies of arms and portrait medallions, all set among small scrolling flower stems recalling those of contemporary Venetian lace. The figure holding a sceptre below a laurel wreath held

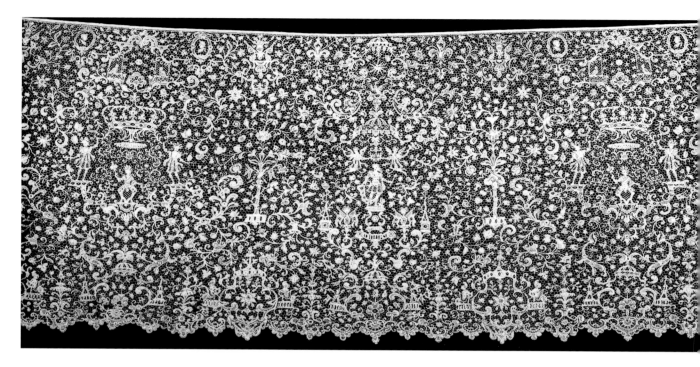

20a. Collar, bobbin lace with a needle-made ground, point d'Angleterre, Belgium, Brussels, Alphonse Nossent, c.1900.
(Reproduced from A. Carlier de Lantsheere, *Les Dentelles à la Main*, Brussels n.d. [c. 1905], pl. 124)

by two putti has been interpreted as Louis XIV himself, especially as a sun appears above his head, but the design also incoporates a small panel with the moon and stars and two owls to represent night, so it may allude to a court masque of some kind. A cravat of c. 1695-1700 in the Cooper-Hewitt Museum in New York also features a figure in theatrical costume under a large crown supported by two putti as the central feature amid various other figures and motifs.[2] The Rijksmuseum piece has been called a flounce for an alb, but the nature of its design makes it far more likely to have been used as a furnishing lace, perhaps round a bed or a toilet-table.

As well as being a masterpiece of its own day, lace of this design has also played a prominent role in the history of collecting. It figured in various European collections in the late 19th century, but in the first half of the 20th century a number of pieces found their way into leading American collections, like those of Isabella Stewart Gardiner in Boston and William A. Clark in Washington.[3] This reflects the dominance of French art in general in many American collections, the lace's French origin and supposed royal connections lending it a special cachet.

It was doubtless the fame of the design that led to copies being made of parts of it in the late 19th century. The central figure with the two putti and a canopy above was adapted around 1900 by the Brussels lace manufacturer Alphonse Nossent, who seems to have specialized in reproduction laces, as the main feature of a large collar in what at that time was called *point d'Angleterre* (for this technique see cat. no. 70), which is described as 'a modern reproduction after a design by Berain' (fig. 20a).[4] In the Boijmans Van Beuningen Museum in Rotterdam there is a late 19th-century flounce in the same technique, which features the secondary figure on the *point de France* flounce under a canopy resembling that of the first, plus a very similar trophy of arms.[5]

1. The story is told in full in Despierres 1886 and Laprade 1905.
2. Sonday 1982, fig. 15.
3. For a full list see Cavallo 1986, cat. no 70. The piece listed there in the collection of Margaret Simeon is now in the Victoria & Albert Museum in London. Not listed there is the piece formerly belonging to Marjory Merriweather Post, which is now in the Hillwood Museum, Washington D.C.
4. Carlier de Lantsheere n.d., pl. 124.
5. *Kant* n.d., cat. no. 37.

21a. Unknown artist in the manner of Willem Wissing (1655-1687), *King-Stadholder William III, c. 1690.* Rijksmuseum Paleis Het Loo

21

CRAVAT END, VENETIAN RAISED NEEDLE LACE, ITALY, VENICE, 1680-1700

---

84 x 26 cm
Inv. no. BK-14216
Provenance: collection of Leopold Iklé; purchased by Mrs L.W. van der Meulen-Nulle; donated by Het Kantsalet, 1927
Literature/Exhibition: Henneberg 1930, fig. 120); Italiaansche Kunst 1934, cat. no. 1203; Van der Meulen-Nulle 1936, fig. 21

Venetian raised needle lace of the heavy variety continued to be made to the end of 17th century, although this cravat end is by no means as heavy as the furnishing flounce cat. no. 15. The piling- up of motifs in the centre reflects influence from contemporary 'candelabrum' patterns, but while the design is symmetrical round this axis, the effect is somewhat lost in the overall swirl of winding stems with flowers and leaves. Indeed, since the cravat ends were bunched together in wear, any strongly symmetrical effect would in any case have been lost. In 1687 James II of England (1685-1688), the father-in-law of Stadholder William III (1650-1702), paid his lace-

man William Rutland £140 for 'Six fine poynt de Venise Cravatts and twelve yardes of fine poynt for Cuffes for our Royall person'.[1] Two years later, William, now joint ruler of England with his wife, Mary II (1689-1694), paid considerably more, £158, for the 'Six point Cravats for our Royall Person', which figure in his first bill from his London seamstresses Judith Radcliffe and Edith Colledge.[2] In all the official portraits painted after his coronation in 1689 William is wearing cravat ends like the Rijksmuseum example and cuffs of the same lace (fig. 21a), while Mary too has neck and sleeve ruffles of heavy Venetian lace in her portraits. The conspicuous expenditure that this represented may be gauged by the fact that 'eight laced hunting Cravats' in the bill of 1689 quoted above cost only £46, presumably because they were trimmed with bobbin lace.

1. Wardle 1997, p. 25.
2. Public Record Office, London, L.C.5 42, fol 29r.

22

PAIR OF CRAVAT ENDS, FLAT VENETIAN NEEDLE LACE, ITALY, VENICE, 1685-1700

Each 17 x 44 cm
Inv. no. BK-16524-A/B
Provenance: collection of Jonkvrouw J.S. Rethaan-Macaré; collection of Mrs E.G. Houwinck; purchased from her by Het Kantsalet; donated by Het Kantsalet to mark its 25th anniversary in 1950, 1951
Literature/Exhibition: Oud-Italiaansche kunst 1934, cat. no. 1196; Erkelens 1965, cat. no. 14; Burgers 1990(2), cat. no. 37

22a. Michiel van Musscher (1645-1705), Hendrick Bicker (1649-1718, Burgomaster of Amsterdam, signed and dated 1682. Inv. no. C 13

been avoided for this purpose, formal or floral ornament being chosen for preference. On this flounce the design, with its many vases and pots of flowers on fantastic stands or brackets and sometimes under canopies, is organized by scrolls into two alternating sections. The flowers include the ever-popular rose, carnation and tulip, while pineapple motifs appear in the border. Shaped panels of formal ornament occur at top and bottom of each section and the lace has a ground of a hexagonal mesh with picots. The motifs are still piled up to some extent in the manner of 'candelabrum' patterns, but this is now less obvious and there is much more movement in the design, so that it probably dates from the early 18th rather than the late 17th century.

This pattern must have been a popular one, as various examples of it survive. There is one in the Musée des Arts Décoratifs in Paris,[1] while another appeared in a sale in 1909.[2] There are also flounces of very similar design in the Musées Royaux d'Art et d'Histoire in Brussels[3] and the Musée des Arts Decoratifs in Paris.[4]

Point de France, though never as fashionable as Venetian lace, was one of the laces that came back into favour towards the end of the 19th century, when many pieces were remodelled and imitations made. At the International Exhibition of 1904 in St Louis, Missouri, for example, Maison Georges Martin, successor to the Compagnie des Indes of Paris and Brussels (see cat. no. 60), gave a 'marvellous flounce of point de France' pride of place in his display, which also included a bertha collar of 'flat' point de France, both pieces made in France.[5] The use of the term flat here suggests a certain confusion or conflation between French and Venetian laces, which is confirmed by an exhibit in the Belgian section: 'a bertha collar in point de Venise, of which the new design, in the manner of point de France, is very interesting and very rich', this piece being made in Belgium.[6]

1. Formerly in the collection of Madame Lionel Normant, Lefébure 1904, fig. 188.
2. Sale of the collection of A. Poloutsoff, 2-4 December 1909, cat. no. 123.
3. Risselin-Steenebrugen 1980, figs. 179, 180.
4. Paris 1983, cat. no. 61, fig. 26.
5. Exposition Internationale de Saint-Louis 1904, p.28.
6. See note 5.

27
BORDER, BOBBIN LACE, SOUTHERN NETHERLANDS, 1700-1725

220 x 7 cm
Inv. no. BK-1958-85
Provenance: purchased by Het Kantsalet from Mrs M. van Smit-van Berckel; donated by Het Kantsalet, 1958
Literature/Exhibition: Burgers 1990(2), cat. no. 43

A masterpiece does not always need to be large and imposing: a delicate border like this also requires considerable mastery for the small-scale pattern to be worked so precisely and made to stand out against the ground. The subtle lines of the scrolling symmetrical motifs reveal the use of whole stitch, half stitch and a decorative filling pattern. The ground here, which was worked at the same time as the pattern, is the relatively simple fond á cinq trous, but these patterns are also found with snowflake and armure grounds.[1]

Lace of this type is sometimes attributed to Binche, sometimes to Antwerp and it was doubtless made in various centres. It was never a fashion lace, but was used on church linen[2] and in the Dutch Republic, Northern Germany[3] and elsewhere, as insertions for pillow covers. It is often found in old Dutch family collections, such as that of the Teding van Berkhout family, which came to the Rijksmuseum with the Six gift,[4] and it provided a good match for the finely woven linen of its time. However, while lace-trimmed bed linen is often listed in Dutch inventories, the type of lace used is seldom or never specified and contemporary advertisements for dealers or sales generally lump bobbin laces together under the generic name 'Brabant' or merely specify the type of ground, such as mesh (spiegeltralie) or bars (stok).

1. Paulis 1947, pl. 42C.
2. Grieten & Bungeneers 1996, no. 863.
3. Preysing 1987, fig. 45.
4. Inv. nos. BK-1978-638, 639, 640.

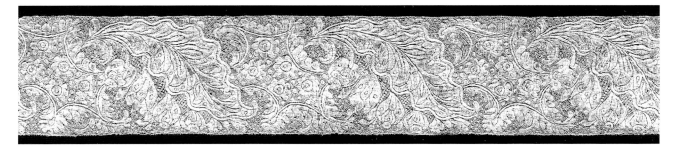

28

BORDER, BINCHE BOBBIN LACE, FRANCE OR SOUTHERN
NETHERLANDS, 1715-1725

---

155 x 8 cm
Inv. no. BK-14653
Provenance: purchased by Het Kantsalet from Mrs L.W. van der Meulen-Nulle;
donated by Het Kantsalet, 1934
Literature/Exhibition: Erkelens 1965, cat. no. 49

At the beginning of the 18th century there was a calami-
tous slump in the lace industry as a result not only of
constant wars, but also of a switch in fashion to plain
muslin accessories. A portrait of Josina Parduyn (1642-
1718) painted by Godfried Schalcken (1643-1706) in 1705

28a. Godfried Schalcken (1643-1706), *Portrait of Josina Parduyn (1642-1718)*, signed
and dated 1705. Inv. no. A 2061

well illustrates this new mode (fig. 28a). Admittedly the
sitter was a widow, but since her husband Aernoud van
Citters (1633-1696) had been ambassador of the Dutch
Republic in London, she must have kept abreast of the
latest fashion in those days and evidently continued to
do so. By the second decade of the century, however, the
bobbin-lace makers of the Southern Netherlands had
begun to produce closely-patterned laces which were
able to compete with muslin in their extraordinary delicacy and refinement, while also having the allure of
intricate design. By this time too the lace-makers were
developing the mesh grounds that were to characterize
their products thenceforth.

This border has a snowflake ground. This has traditionally been linked with Binche, but doubt has now been
cast on the association of this type of lace with that
town. From the 1740s onwards it is known for certain
that the lace-makers of Binche were producing motifs
for Brussels bobbin lace.[1] Thus it seems more likely that
this earlier type of lace was made at Valenciennes, where
the industry had begun to revive by around 1720, and
perhaps also at the other centres that produced lace of
the Valenciennes type, such as Ghent or Enghien.
However, the term 'Binche' so usefully covers this type
of lace, in which pattern and ground often seem merged
together, that it seems advisable to retain it with the
above-mentioned proviso, particularly as the extent to
which other types of lace denoted by the names of towns
were also made elsewhere has now become clear.

The design of this border, with its slanting movement,
is related to that of the 'luxuriant Bizarre' woven silks of
the second decade of the 18th century. The large leaves
and fruits are typical of this style, as are the oddly-
shaped 'cartouches' with their floral pattern.[2]

1. Risselin-Steenebrugen 1956, p. 221; Coppens 1996.
2. Cf. Thornton 1965, pl. 44a; Levey 1983, fig. 300.

29

FLOUNCE FOR AN ALB (INCOMPLETE), NEEDLE LACE, POINT DE
FRANCE, FRANCE, 1715-1725

200 x 60 cm
Inv. no. BK-14523
Provenance: originally part of a complete alb flounce in the collection of Alfred Lescure;
purchased by Mrs L.W. van der Meulen-Nulle; this half purchased by Het Kantsalet
(the other by the Musées Royaux d'Art et d'Histoire, Brussels¹), 1931;
donated by Het Kantsalet, 1931
Literature/Exhibition: Cox 1908, p. 29, no. 31; Meulen-Nulle 1936, fig. 28;
Oude Kant 1938, cat. no. 104; Erkelens 1965, cat. no. 18

This flounce, which also has a ground of a hexagonal mesh with picots, seems to represent a rather later development in design than cat. no. 26. The pattern is still organized in two alternating sections, but the scrolls demarcating them are now much less distinct, so that everything seems to merge into an overall rich effect. Flower-vase motifs are still present, but have also assumed a less clearly defined and sometimes rather strange appearance.

Grand flounces like this for ecclesiastical use contributed very substantially to keeping the industries at Alençon and Argentan in being during the slump in the lace industry in the early 18th century. Not very much seems to be known in detail about developments in Alençon, but at Argentan the leading manufacturer shortly after the beginning of the 18th century was Mathieu Guyard (see also cat. no. 35), who was granted the royal privilege in 1708 for the industry founded by his father.[2] In his petition for the privilege Guyard had stated, so a later document repeats,[3] that lace making in Argentan had utterly collapsed, but although the industry doubtless had suffered badly during the slump, this may have been something of an exaggeration. Guyard employed as his designer Pierre Montulay (d. 1741), *dessinateur graveur*, but in 1714 the two men parted company and Montulay started a rival business of his own. He was granted the royal privilege in that year and proved no less successful. In his request for a second renewal of the privilege in 1733 he related how he employed four to five hundred workers and had had 'the honour of making the cravats and collars of Her Majesty, even those she had used during her coronation', as well as 'the bed coverlet for the marriage of the King' (Louis XV had come of age and married Maria Leczinska in 1723).[4] Montulay must have been one of the small number of

47

manufacturers who actually made their own designs. After he left Mathieu Guyard's firm he was replaced as director there by Jacques James, while the new designer was Louis Mignan, who in his turn was succeeded some time before 1726 by Mathieu Denis Manceau.[5]

1. Inv. D.1066, Paulis 1935, fig. 26; Risselin-Steenebrugen, n.d., p. 13, pl. XII; idem 1980, fig. 182.
2. Laprade 1908, p. 109.
3. Ibid. p. 123.
4. Ibid. pp. 110, 111-112, 115.
5. Ibid., p. 122.

30

CAP BACK AND LAPPETS, BRUSSELS BOBBIN LACE, SOUTHERN NETHERLANDS, 1715-1725

Cap back: 23 x 27 cm; lappets: 58 x 11.5 cm
Inv. no. BK-1965-3-A/B/C
Provenance: collection of Mrs M. May-Polak Daniëls; collection of Mrs E. van Marx-May collection of R. May; purchased by Het Kantsalet from
J. Post; donated by Het Kantsalet on its 40th anniversary, 1965
Literature/Exhibition: Hollandsch Interieur 1931, cat. no. 226; Oude Kant 1938, cat. nos. 31, 32; Erkelens 1965, cat. no. 45; Burgers 1990(2), cat. no. 50

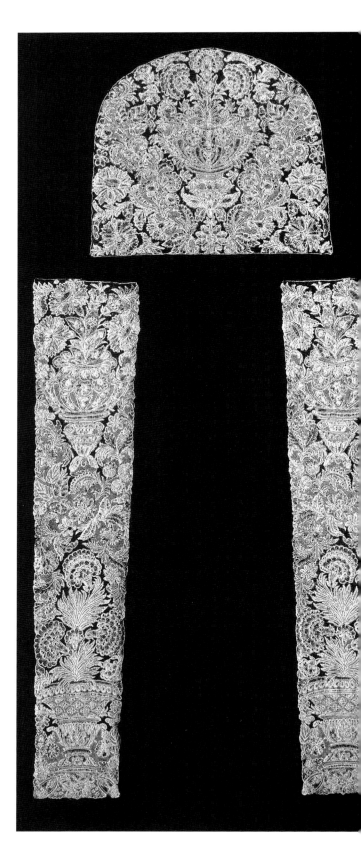

These magnificent components of a cap are an outstanding masterpiece of lace design and bobbin-lace making, revealing the heights the Flemish industry was able to reach as it emerged from the slump of the early 18th century. The design, which occupies the major part of the space available, is organized around a series of large flower vases. These have been called 'garden vases' ever since the pieces entered the Rijksmuseum's collection. Yet, only the vase at the bottom of the lappets fits that description and even it is actually more reminiscent of silverwork, especially in respect of the elaborate ornamentation of the foot, the acanthus leaves and fluting at the base of the bowl and the gadrooning round the rim. The other two vases on the lappets and the one on the cap back are much more exotic in character, appearing to rise out of a sort of chalice and decorated round the top with floral scallops. The flowers in the vases are of an exotic type common in Indian chintz designs of the period,[1] which also figure on Meissen and other porcelain from c. 1725 onwards as 'Indianische Blumen' or 'Fleurs des Indes'.[2] The flower patterns inside the leaves in the upper vases on the lappets are another feature found in chintz design, as well as some contemporary quilting patterns.

The high quality and richness of this design are indicative of the skills of a first-rate designer, most probably a Parisian. Two more Brussels lappets formerly in the collection of Alfred Lescure are comparable in style and may well be by the same hand (fig. 30a). One of them features a silver covered bowl, with its lid open to reveal flowers,

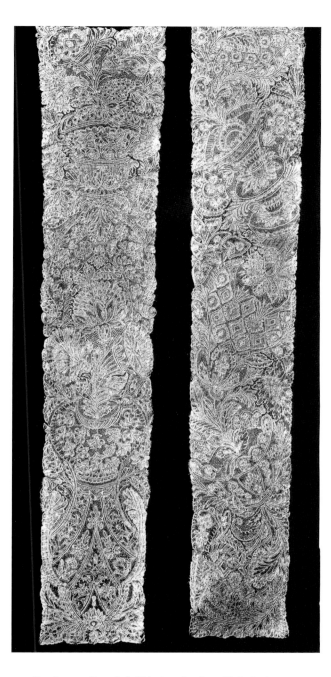

tives of the grander designs, while undoubtedly also owing something to bizarre silk patterns.[3]

The motifs have the raised edge characteristic of Brussels lace from this time onwards, while the main ground, which was worked around them later, is of the hexagonal form which had already evolved by the end of the 17th century. Some of the floral motifs also have a fancy ground of their own. The whole effect is extraordinarily rich, while the fineness of the thread gives the lace a remarkable delicacy.

1. Cf. Hartkamp-Jonxis 1987, cat. nos. 107 and 112, and Irwin & Brett 1970, figs. 19, 23, 30, cat. nos. 14, 15, 18, all dated early or first half of the 18th century.
2. I am indebted to Ebeltje Hartkamp-Jonxis for the information on the 'Indianische Blumen', for which see Fleming & Honour 1989.
3. See, for example, Risselin-Steenebrugen 1980, fig. 278; Coppens 1981, cat. no. 20; Carmigiani & Fossi Todorow 1981, cat. no. 58; Levey 1983, figs 299 a,b (the latter a Valenciennes lappet).

31
FLOUNCE, NEEDLE LACE, POINT DE FRANCE, FRANCE, 1720-1725

---

270 x 66 cm
Inv. no. BK-1966-86
Provenance: purchased from art-dealer Madame L. Collette-Payre, Paris; donated by the Commissie voor Fotoverkoop, 1966
Literature/Exhibition: Modes et Dentelles 1983, cat. no. 68; Burgers 1990(2), cat. no. 38

French needle lace of this type has been referred to in the past as *point de Sedan*, but while the town of Sedan was one of those where the making of both needle and bobbin lace was introduced or stimulated by Colbert's Ordinance of 1665, it is impossible to identify any of the lace that was made there. In any case, it seems likely that the needle lace industry never developed to the same extent there as in Alençon and Argentan.[1] The fineness of the thread in this piece and the abundance of filling patterns has led to the suggestion that this and other similar examples may have been made in the Southern Netherlands, but there is no way of ascertaining this at our present state of knowledge.[2]

The closely-packed design with many elaborate leaves, pineapple-like fruit and palmette motifs is organized around a central section surmounted by curved bands of patterned strapwork and a pendant shell motif, elements often found in silver design at this period.[3] Many other features of the design are also found, sometimes equally closely packed together, in woven silks of the same time,[4] while conspicuous diaper filling patterns like those in the scrolls and fruit entered woven silk design in the 1710s and became common in the 1720s.[5] A *point de France* flounce in the Metropolitan Museum of Art, New York, exhibits a comparable mixture of exotic motifs and asymmetry.[6]

30a. Two lappets, Brussels bobbin lace, Southern Netherlands 1715-1725. Formerly in the collection of Alfred Lescure. (Reproduced from E. Overloop, *Matériaux pour servir á l'histoire de la dentelle en Belgique. Troisième Serie, Dentelles Anciennes de la Collection Alfred Lescure*, Brussels 1914, pl.VII left and centre)

and an exotic bowl on a stand, the other a monteith-like silver bowl and a container composed of an interlinked series of funnel shapes. Similar exotic flowers combined with less conspicuous funnel or vase forms appear on many lappets of this period and may perhaps be deriva-

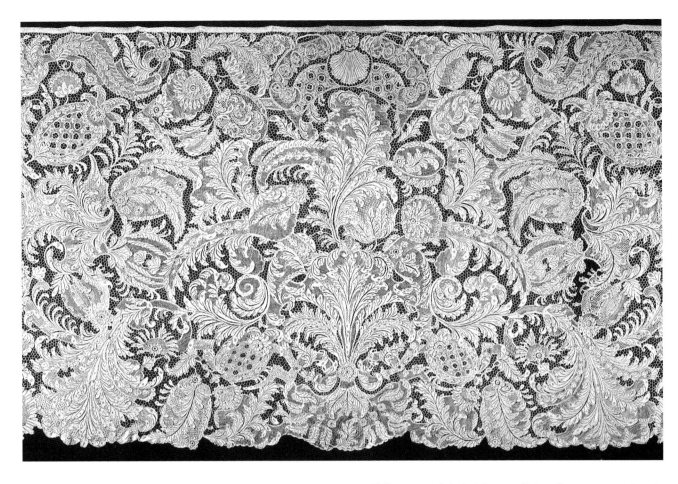

31a. Collar, composed of *point de France* needle lace of c. 1720-1730, made up in the latter part of the 19th century. Donated by Het Kantsalet in 1988. Inv. no BK-1988-30

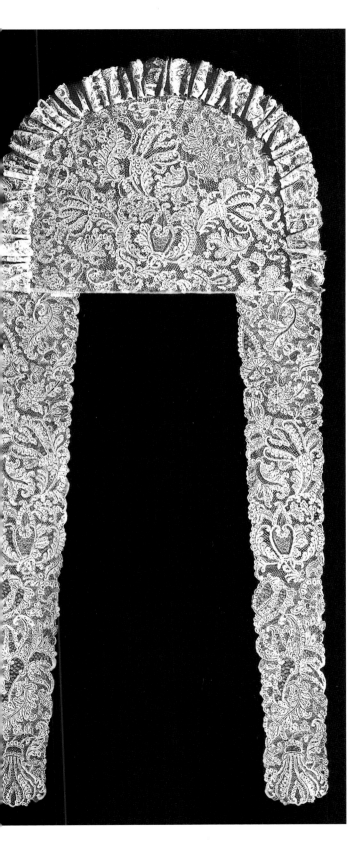

Like Venetian needle lace, this type of *point de France* enjoyed a renewed popularity at the end of the 19th century, not only as a collector's item, but also for fashionable wear. The Rijksmuseum's collection includes a collar composed of parts of a *point de France* flounce or flounces, which formerly belonged to successive members of the De Constant Rebecque family, several members of which figured prominently in court circles (fig. 31a).[7]

1. Levey 1983, p. 54.
2. Risselin-Steenebrugen 1980, p. 251; Modes et Dentelles 1983, cat. no. 68.
3. See, for example, the many designs on the six large sheets Nouveau Desseins pour graver sur l'orfevrerie. Inventés et gravés par le Sieur Masson, which were published in Paris in the early 18th century by J.Mariette. Masson was a French goldsmith and engraver.
4. See, for example, Thornton 1965, pls. 44B and 56A.
5. Rothstein, 1999, figs. 172, 173.
6. Levey 1983, fig. 171.
7. The collar was exhibited in Haarlem in 1903, see Naber 1903, Pl. VI.

32

CAP BACK, LAPPETS AND BORDER, NEEDLE LACE, FRANCE, 1720-1730

Cap back: 22 x 29 cm; lappets 57 x 9.5 cm; border: 146 x 5 cm
Inv. no. BK-1962-31
Provenance: purchased by Het Kantsalet from Madame A. Bernard, Paris, a member of a family of Dutch descent; donated by Het Kantsalet, 1962
Literature/Exhibition: Erkelens 1965, cat. no. 23

These cap components, in shapes that were to remain in vogue with only minor variations until the 1780s, are typical of the accessories produced in the 1720s, when needle lace began to return to the fashion scene. The French needle-lace makers did their best to emulate the closely-packed designs of Flemish bobbin lace, but their product lacked the muslin-like fineness of the Flemish lace, so that this lace inevitably looks rather heavy by comparison. The design of the cap back has an asymmetry comparable to that in cat. no. 31 of the same period, as well as some similar leaf shapes, while the flower forms exhibit a comparable exoticism.

The purchase by J.B. Godefroy of Brussels in 1719 of a complete set of *point de France* accessories,[1] including a cap, indicates how keen the Brussels lace manufacturers were to emulate the French, albeit they soon abandoned the French model in favour of a kind of needle lace made with their own much finer thread (see cat. no. 37).

1. Risselin-Steenebrugen 1956, p. 223.

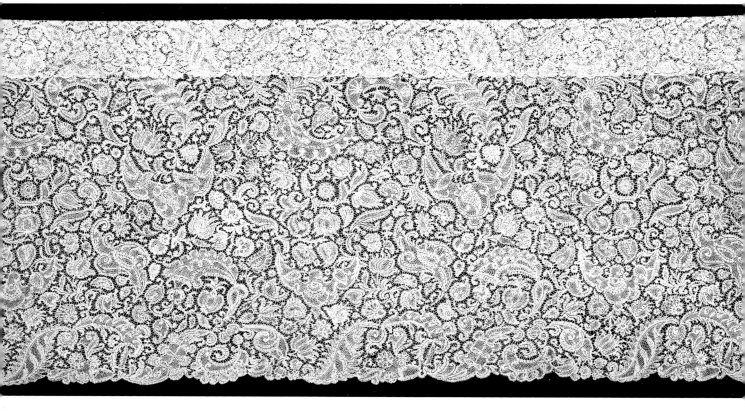

33
FLOUNCE AND BORDER, BRUSSELS BOBBIN LACE, SOUTHERN NETHERLANDS, 1720-1730

140 x 72 cm
Inv. no. BK-NM-13229
Provenance: donated by Het Kantsalet, 1925
Literature/Exhibition: Oude Kant 1938, cat. no. 37; Erkelens 1965, cat. 46;
Wardle 1996, p. 32

This flounce of Brussels bobbin lace was the first gift made to the Rijksmuseum by Het Kantsalet. It has a border attached to it along the top edge. A slightly wider flounce of the same design with the same border attached along the top, now in the collection of the Gruuthusemuseum at Bruges, may originally have belonged with the Rijksmuseum lace.[1] The presence of the border suggests that these pieces were originally the flounce and border of a toilet-table cover. Until about 1730 the drapery or 'petticoat' was confined to the toilet-table itself, but after that a 'scarf' was added over the mirror.[2]

The closely-packed design of this lace illustrates how well the Brussels lace designers were able to adapt the patterns of contemporary woven silks. Similar leaf shapes and rather bizarre formal ornament can be seen in some English silk designs of the 1720s,[3] while comparable motifs, including very similar tulip-like flowers, are also found in a Brussels lace Benediction veil in the Musées Royaux d'Art et d'Histoire in Brussels, which is dated 1720.[4] Like the Rijksmuseum lace, this last piece has a ground of bars rather than mesh, the two types of ground continuing to be used side by side until around 1750.[5] A flounce with a design very close to that in the Rijksmuseum was formerly in an English collection.[6]

1. Inv. O.140.XIX. Vandenberghe et al 1990, cat. no. 365. The measurements given there are 151 x 71 cm.
2. Wardle 1996, p. 32.
3. Rothstein 1990, figs. 54 (1721), 57 (c. 1726).
4. Risselin-Steenebrugen 1980, fig. 283.
5. Levey 1983, p. 46.
6. Simeon 1979, pl. 62.

34
PAIR OF LAPPETS, MECHLIN BOBBIN LACE, SOUTHERN NETHERLANDS, 1720-1730

62 x 11 cm
Inv. no. BK-1955-109
Provenance: purchased at sale Amsterdam (Frederik Muller), 8-15 November 1955, no. 1024
Literature/Exhibition: Burgers 1990(2), cat. no. 47

bin laces are the most beautiful after Brussels and last rather longer',[5] this extra strength presumably being owed to the straight lace technique, where no joins were involved.

1. Risselin-Steenebrugen 1975, pp. 212, 215, 217.
2. Levey 1983, p.47.
3. Seligman 1923.
4. See note 2 and Risselin-Steenebrugen 1975, p. 208.
5. Cited in Dreger 1910, p. 130.

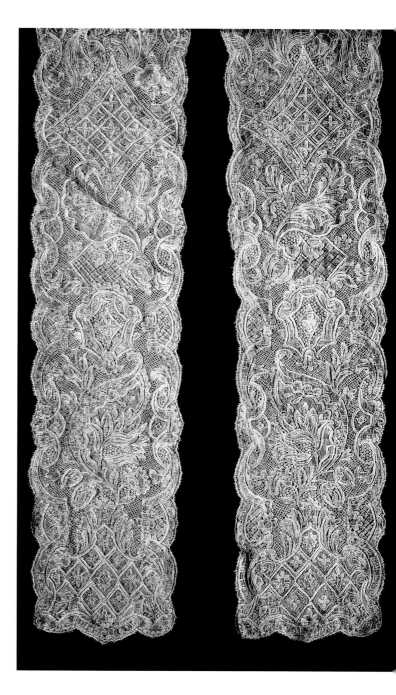

Lace making at Mechelen (anglicized as Mechlin in referring to the lace) goes back to the second half of the 16th century. The principal lace merchant there at that time, Jehan de Raighers, supplied the Plantin firm in Antwerp not only with cutwork and needle lace, but also with 'passemans' [trimmings] and 'dantelles', a reference to the latter of 1578 seeming to mark the introduction of this new term for bobbin lace.[1] Later, from the mid-17th century onwards, the name Mechlin or Malines often occurs in juxtaposition with *point d'Angleterre*, the current name for Brussels bobbin lace, so the inference would seem to be that it was a generic name for straight lace, i.e. lace made all in one piece, motifs and ground together, as opposed to part lace in which the motifs are made first and the ground worked round them afterwards.[2] The two terms 'point d'Angleterre' and 'Malines' are found as late as 1720 in the inventory of the wardrobe of Marie Anne de Bourbon, Princesse de Condé (1689-1720), where they are used for the finest lace in her possession.[3] However, in general in the 18th century the term 'Mechlin' signifies a straight lace in which the motifs are outlined by a thicker thread or *cordonet*. At first it had various kinds of mesh ground (the 1720 inventory cited above speaks of it *à reseau* and *à-brides*), including the snowflake ground of so-called Binche lace.

The sophisticated pattern of these lappets must have came from a designer in Brussels, if not in Paris. It is comparatively static, incorporating lozenges and shaped panels of filling patterns and smaller cartouche-like forms arranged vertically with more exuberant sprigs of flowers, fruit and leaves between them and borders of formal ornament. The ground, a simple *fond à cinq trous*, occupies only a small area.

Little is known as yet of the history of the lace industry in Mechelen itself, but in 1681 a visitor to the town already commented on the prominent part played by the Béguinage (one of the early suppliers of the Plantin firm was a Béguine) and in 1724 another traveller, John Macky, noted that it was there that 'they make the best Mechlin lace'.[4] In 1723 Savory des Bruslons noted in his Dictionnaire universel de commerce that 'Mechlin bob-

35

SLEEVE RUFFLE (INCOMPLETE), ALENÇON NEEDLE LACE, FRANCE,
1725-1735

———

117 x 14 cm
Inv. no. BK-1970-200
Provenance: purchased from Mrs L.W. van der Meulen-Nulle by Mrs A. Jiskoot-Pierson, a
former President of Het Kantsalet, 1934; bequeathed to Het Kantsalet, 1970; donated by
Het Kantsalet, 1970
Literature/Exhibition: Erkelens 1970, cat. no. 40; Burgers 1990(2), cat. no. 43

This sleeve ruffle is in the shape characteristic of what was an indispensable fashion accessory for much of the 18th century, with a symmetrical design starting in the wide centre and tapering off towards the ends. It dates from the period before the characteristic Alençon mesh ground (see cat. no. 50) became standardized around 1750 and exhibits the use of a variety of fancy filling patterns as part of the ground.[1] Part of a ruffle of the same design illustrated in Auguste Lefébure's book of 1904

35a. Johann Valentin Tischbein (1715-1768), attributed to, *Anne of Hanover* (1709-1749), signed and dated 1753. Inv. no. A

35b. Guillaume de Spinny (1721-1768), *Wilhelmina of Prussia* (1751-1820), dated 1775. Inv. no. A 4927

has a rather heavier basic ground and is there called *point de Sedan*[2] (for this name see cat. no. 31). The design of large flowers and leaves emerging from a central plant form is fairly close-packed, indicating a date of around 1725 to 1735.

The types of lace now distinguished as Alençon and Argentan appear to have been made at both towns. Among the leading manufacturers at Alençon around 1730 were François Marescot, who was described in a lawsuit of 1731 as 'merchant in *Points de France* at Paris, proprietor of a business for the manufacture of these types of needle lace established at Alençon', and Jacques-Pierre D'Ocagne, a member of a dynasty of *maîtres dentelliers* extending from the early 17th to the mid-19th century, whose son Jacques-René Benjamin was the first to establish himself in Paris in the mid-18th century.[3] In Argentan the principal manufacturer was still Mathieu Guyard, *marchand mercier à Paris*, who had been granted the royal privilege in 1708. In petitions for its renewal in 1726 he remarked that he had now reached the age of 73 and was bowed down by infirmities, requesting that it be extended after him to his sons Claude Simon, aged 28, and Louis François, aged 26, whom he had imbued from their infancy with the knowledge needed for the business.[4] Guyard, who also owned a lace firm in the Paris region and produced silk as well as linen lace, employed as designers first Louis Mignan of Paris and later

Mathieu Denis Manceau, whose brothers Jacques-Michel and Joachim-Joseph were likewise designers.[5] Evidently the designing of lace, like its manufacture, could run in families.

French needle lace continued to be *de rigueur* for court dress until late in the 18th century (see also cat. no. 50). In their official portraits of 1753 and 1775 respectively Anne of Hanover (1709-1759), consort of Stadholder William IV (1711-1751), and Wilhelmina of Prussia (1751-1820), consort of William V (1748-1806), are wearing elaborate sleeve ruffles of this lace in the increasingly open patterns fashionable in those years (figs. 35a,b).

1. Cf. Kraatz 1992, nos. 66 and 67.
2. Lefébure 1904, fig. 180.
3. De Laprade 1905, pp. 96, 98.
4. Ibid., p. 125.
5. Ibid., pp. 123, 125.

36

FLOUNCE, ARGENTAN NEEDLE LACE, FRANCE, 1725-1735

360 x 64 cm
Inv. no. BK-16004
Provenance: purchased by Mrs C. Visser-Wertheim from an art-dealer in Paris, 1938; donated by Het Kantsalet, 1946
Literature/Exhibition: Erkelens 1965, cat. no. 21; Burgers 1990(2), cat. no. 2

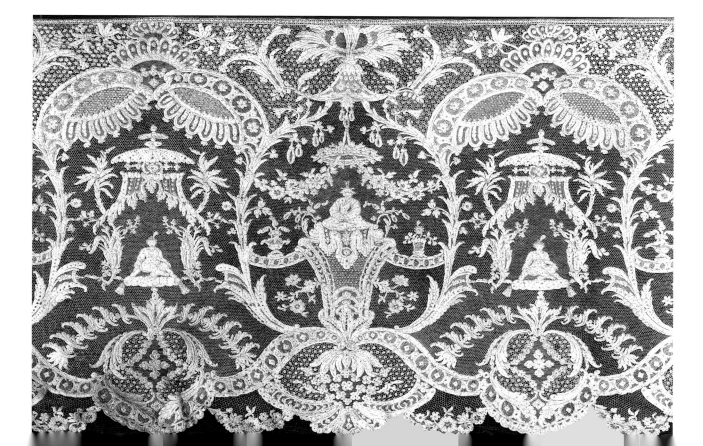

36a. Flounce, needle lace with a Brussels point de gaze ground, Belgium, last quarter of the 19th century. (Reproduced from A. Carlier de Lantsheere, *Trésors de l'art dentellier*, Brussels 1922, pl. 83).

No contemporary parallel seems to exist for this heavy needle lace flounce, which has the hexagonal, button-holed mesh ground usually associated with Argentan in two different sizes. It does, however, seem to belong in a range of designs with comparable elements. The designer may well have been familiar with the first tapestry in a set woven in Beauvais called *La Teinture chinoise*, which features a seated Chinese figure under a heavy canopy. This set, which probably dates from around 1700, was rewoven up to 1731.[1] Similarly, an engraving of a *Divinité chinoise* of c. 1709 after Antoine Watteau (1684-1721) shows a figure seated cross-legged on a raised dais in a setting with a canopy, trees and various ornaments,[2] while the wreath with garlands suspended through it, the husk ornament and the curved stems with stylized leaves in the lace likewise figure among Watteau's repertoire. Some of the ornament is also found in a group of very distinctive *point de France* flounces sometimes said to be in the style of Daniel Marot.[3] The identical flounces in the Victoria & Albert Museum in London and the Abegg Stiftung at Riggisberg further feature a cover in three scalloped parts like the one on which the higher of the two figures in the lace is seated. The *point de France* flounces are all dated early in the 18th century, but ornament of types comparable to that on the Rijksmuseum flounce can also be seen on later *point de France* and Argentan flounces exhibited in Paris in 1906.[4] The comparative openness of the design of the Rijksmuseum piece puts it at around

1725 to 1735. Flounces of lace are recorded in 18th-century inventories as having been used around beds, so perhaps this one figured in a Chinoiserie room around a bed with hangings in a similar style, like the North Italian set at the Abegg Stiftung.[5] Alternatively it may have adorned a toilet-table. That it was certainly highly valued is evinced by the many repairs that have been made to it, unusually, in silk thread. The design of this lace must once have been a well-known one, since quite close reproductions were made of it in the late 19th century. Carlier de Lantsheere illustrates a flounce in needle lace with a *point de gaze* ground (fig. 36a),[6] while in the Museum Boijmans Van Beuningen in Rotterdam there is a sample of the same design in the *point d'Angleterre* of that time, i.e. bobbin lace with a *point de gaze* ground (see cat. no. 70).

1. Jarry 1981, p. 16.
2. Dacier & Vuaflart 1929, Vol. I, no. 134, Vol. II, p. 27.
3. Levey 1983, fig. 176 (Victoria & Albert Museum); Gruber 1985 no. 5 (Abegg Stiftung); Kraatz 1992, fig. 22 under cat. no 61 (Textile Museum, St Gallen).
4. Exposition Paris 1906, nos. 9 and 11.
5. Gruber 1984, no. 27.
6. Carlier de Lantsheere 1922, pl. 83. The flounce is said to be in the Musées Royaux d'Art et d'Histoire, but it is not there now. Information kindly supplied by Marguerite Coppens.
7. Inv. M. 199, formerly in the collection of W.H. de Monchy, Rotterdam.

37

BORDER, BRUSSELS NEEDLE LACE, SOUTHERN NETHERLANDS, 1730-1740

100 x 10.5 cm
Inv. no. BK-16438-B
Provenance: purchased by Het Kantsalet from Mrs L.W. van der Meulen-Nulle; donated by Het Kantsalet, 1939
Literature/Exhibition: Erkelens 1955, fig. 26; Erkelens 1965, cat. no. 25; Burgers 1990(2), cat. no 39

40a. Frans van der Mijn (1719-1784), *Portrait of Maria Henriette van de Poll (1707-1787)*, dated by the costume to 1740-1750. Inv. no. A 1274

40b. Henriette Wolters-van Pee (1692-1741), *Self Portrait*, miniature, dated 1732 by an inscription on the back. Inv. no. A 2410

different design, but nothing is known as to when or where this was added. Normally the frill round the front of the cap was of the same pattern as the lappets and crown. In the 1730s and 1740s it was often worn with a conspicuous dip at centre front (fig. 40a), while the lappets could either hang loosely down the back or be pinned up on top of the head (fig. 40b).

1. Risselin-Steenebrugen 1956, p. 225.
2. Rothstein 1990, pl. 244, lower fig. on p. 234 and figs on p. 238, the first dated 1748, the others 1749.

41
LAPPET, BRUSSELS BOBBIN LACE, SOUTHERN NETHERLANDS, 1740-1750

63 x 12 cm
Inv. no. BK-1975-373
Provenance: collection of Baroness M. van der Feltz-van der Feltz;
donated by Het Kantsalet to mark its golden jubilee, 1975
Literature/Exhibition: Burgers 1990(2), cat. no. 51

Only diagonally placed flower sprigs offer any movement in the design of this lappet, giving the effect of a division into compartments. Most of the flowers themselves are in a straight alignment like the sprigs at top and bottom and in the centre, which spring from shaped panels decorated with filling patterns. Various filling patterns are also incorporated in the motifs, while much of the ground is left visible.

The names of four lace designers in Brussels around this period are preserved in the records of the Godfrey-Du Rondeau firm of that city: F.J. Dutrieu, J. Fr. Decoster, Keustet or Keuster and Quenixloot or Conixloot.[1] The best of these seems to have been Dutrieu, who supplied designs to the firm for over twenty years. Keuster was also among the five designers from whom the Brussels lace-merchant Caroline d'Halluin bought designs.[2] The fame of Brussels designers even spread as far as Valenciennes. Caroline d'Halluin's accounts further yield the names of other lace specialists in Brussels: Elena Vermoute, *tireuse de patron*, whose task was to make a sample piece of lace from the original design as a guide to the lace-makers, and four women by the names of Dounckers, Laderier, Scoinnatte and Catoir, to whom was entrusted the delicate task of uniting the separate parts to form the complete design. Their work naturally depended on the skill of the lace-makers themselves, who had to work to the same tension in order to secure the success of the design as a whole. All this serves as a reminder of the complex processes involved in the creation of this most sought-after lace.

1. Risselin-Steenebrugen 1956, pp. 216, 218.
2. Risselin-Steenebrugen 1957, p. 6.

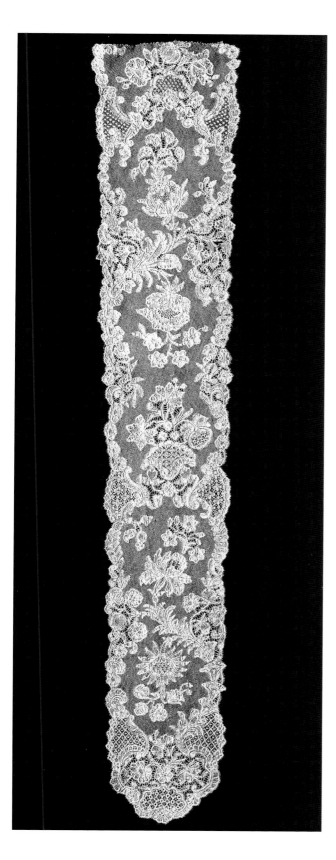

56 x 11 cm
Inv. no. BK-1958-120
Provenance: acquired from the collection of Z. Falkowski, Chicago;
donated by the Commissie voor Fotoverkoop, 1958

42a. Jan Jacob Nachenius (1709-1752?), *Portrait of Jacoba Maria van Bueren gezegd van Regteren (1718-1791)*, signed and dated 1746. Inv. no. A 1657

These lappets have the hexagonal mesh ground commonly associated with Mechlin lace, which gradually superseded other kinds of ground towards the middle of the 18th century. The formal ornament is now less prominent than in cat. no. 38, while it still lends liveliness to the design with its prominent diagonal movement. The flowers and fruit have become more realistic, with daffodil, pomegranate and currants recognizable among them. As in cat. no. 38 the sprigs have their own little background of a spotted filling pattern. A similar design can be seen on the sleeve ruffles in a portrait of 1746 (fig. 42a)

In the mid-18th century Mechlin lace was the second most important type after Brussels to be supplied by the Godefroy-Du Rondeau firm in Brussels.[1] Godefroy procured some Mechlin lace at Ypres and Menin, but the firm's chief suppliers in the 1740s appear to have been Anna De Ridder and a woman by the name of Devijler, both possibly factors, and Mlle Camion, a Béguine.[2] Another Mechelen lace-merchant around 1750 was Joanna Melaen, from whom Caroline d'Halluin of Brussels got her supplies.[2]

1. Risselin-Steenebrugen 1956, pp. 225-226.
2. Idem., p. 229.
3. Risselin-Steenebrugen 1957, p. 9.

43
LAPPET, BINCHE BOBBIN LACE, FRANCE OR SOUTHERN NETHERLANDS, 1745-1755

55 x 9 cm
Inv. no. BK-1971-100
Provenance: collection of Mrs M.E. Leopold Siemens-Ruyter; bequeathed to Mrs A.M.L.E. Mulder-Erkelens, 1971; donated to the Rijksmuseum, 1971

The flower sprigs in this refined design are contained within an interlocking series of shaped panels surrounded by formal flowers and leaves. Each of the sprigs bears two different flowers, one of which resembles a tulip, while the others are unrecognizable. This design is set against a snowflake ground with some small areas of *fond à cinq trous*.

A Binche lappet of similar design in the Musées Royaux d'Art et d'Histoire in Brussels has an even more fanciful outline.[1] Some of the floral motifs on it also resemble those on the Rijksmuseum lappet. Another set of Binche lappets in the same collection has a similar design of flowers in panels, but here the panels are outlined by narrow bands, while carnations and marguerites, as well as tulips, can be recognized among the flowers.[2] The parallels and differences between these designs illustrate the remarkable fact that one seldom or never comes across two sets of lappets of identical design, certainly not in the first half of the 18th century. Lappets and their matching cap backs seem to have challenged lace designers to apply what was evidently an inexhaustible stream of invention.

1. Van Overloop 1911-1912, pl. LX left.
2. Ibid, pl. LX right; Coppens 1981, cat. no. 76.

44
FURNISHING FLOUNCE, BRUSSELS BOBBIN LACE, SOUTHERN NETHERLANDS, 1750-1760

130 x 60 cm
Inv. no. BK-BR-J-218-A
Provenance: on loan from the Koninklijke Verzamelingen,
The Hague, 1966
Literature/Exhibition: Erkelens & Burgers 1966, cat. no. 171; Levey 1983, fig. 333;
Wardle 1996, pp. 33-34

This lace, with its bold arrangement of sprays of flowers and leaves within a framework of patterned scrolls interlaced with garlands of flowers, displays the greater openness that came into lace design around the middle of the 18th century. Designs like this inspired the exuberant combinations of flowers and patterned bands that were to be so popular in the third quarter of the 19th century (cat. no. 61), albeit the flowers here are mostly of an exotic variety with little of the naturalism that was to be so dominant in the 19th century.

Although similar designs also appear in dress flounces in the mid-18th century, the weight of this one shows without doubt that it was used for furnishing purposes. The 1759 inventory of Anne of Hanover lists two toilet-table flounces and two bed valances of Brussels lace, which may well have looked like this.[1] No mention is made there of the lining of the lace, but evidence from paintings and inventories suggests that pink and crimson were favourite colours for toilet-tables. In a portrait of c. 1765 by Johann Zoffany (1734/5-1810), Queen Charlotte of England (1744-1818) is shown seated beside her dressing table, which is draped with fine lace lined and tied with bows of crimson silk.[2] In 1767 the trousseau of Wilhelmina of Prussia included 'A toilet-table cover of Brussels lace lined with green taffeta', green being her favourite colour.[3]

1. Wardle 1991, p. 32.
2. Idem, p. 31.
3. Koninklijk Huisarchief, The Hague, 315 A 32.

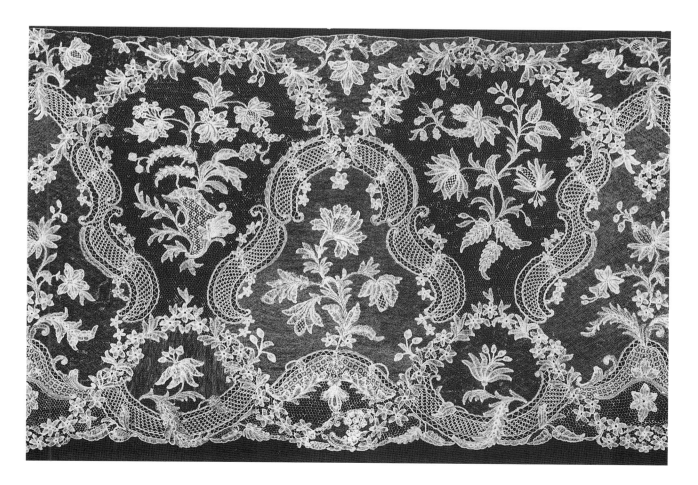

45

PAIR OF LAPPETS, VALENCIENNES BOBBIN LACE, FRANCE OR
SOUTHERN NETHERLANDS, 1750-1760

103 x 10 cm
Inv. no. BK-NM-14101
Provenance: donated by Miss M. de Monchy, 1926

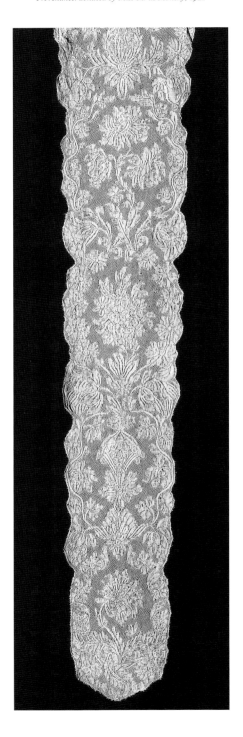

45a. Daniel Bruyninx (1724-1787), *Portrait of a Woman,* miniature, signed and
dated 1764. Inv. no. A 4785

Valenciennes was not the most fashionable of laces. It
was generally considered more suitable for négligé wear,
especially as it washed so well with its strong mesh
ground plaited on all four sides and its solid designs
entirely in whole stitch. The design of this lappet dates
it to the 1750s, when much more of the ground was
becoming visible. Formal ornament has now disappeared from the borders, while the central field is divi-
ded into compartments outlined by delicate stems or
rows of flowers. Large flowers dominate the rather static
central sprigs, but only the tulips rising from a vase-like
form are recognizable. A slightly later version of this
type of design can be seen in a miniature of an unknown
sitter dated 12 April 1764 (fig. 45a). This portrait also
shows another way of wearing the cap, with the frill
upright and the lappets carried over the back of the
head, brought forward beside the cheeks and fastened
under the chin.

During the prosperous period from c. 1740 to the mid-
1770s the leading firm among the twenty or so at
Valenciennes (which had passed into French hands in
1678) was that begun by François-Joseph Tribout and
his wife Anne Cécile Dannezaan soon after their marria-

ge in 1746[1] and later continued by their daughter Claire. This firm had its main contacts in Paris and Brussels and relations as far afield as Amsterdam, Vienna, Italy and London. To Tribout, along with Mlle Reine-Esther Taverne, who eventually became superior of the Convent des Orphelines in the town, was owed the perfecting of the Valenciennes technique. Mlle Taverne made the best and most beautiful lappets and was thus entrusted with Tribout's most important orders.[2] He paid great attention to design, stressing that it must be 'of the latest and most novel taste', when he wrote to his correspondent in Brussels, Mlle Lebrun, asking her to buy designs from the best designer there for him.[3] He bought designs in Paris as well.

Lace in the Valenciennes technique was also made at various places in the Southern Netherlands. Caroline d'Halluin obtained supplies from Ghent,[4] Jean-Baptiste Godefroy from Ghent and Enghien,[5] and there were a number of other centres.

1. Guignet 1979, p. 99.
2. Malotet 1927, p. 35.
3. Idem, p. 30.
4. Risselin-Steenebrugen 1957, p. 9.
5. Risselin-Steenebrugen 1956, p. 220.

46
SLEEVE RUFFLE, BRUSSELS BOBBIN LACE, SOUTHERN NETHERLANDS, 1760-1770

---

95 x 8.5 cm
Inv. no. BK-1958-122
Provenance: collection of Z. Falkowski, Chicago; donated by the Commissie voor Fotoverkoop, 1958
Literature/Exhibition: Burgers 1990(2), cat. no. 54

After 1750 lace became much lighter in design. In a letter of 31 March 1763 from Paris Jean-Baptiste Godefroy, the Paris agent of the Godefroy-Du Rondeau firm in Brussels, wrote of 'sleeve ruffles of a new design, neither overloaded nor with large flowers'.[1] The new trend is illustrated by this ruffle, in which a decorative band undulating from side to side divides the field into compartments containing flowers, a large part of the mesh ground being left undecorated. Rococo cartouches still appear along the edge, but are much reduced in size, while the use of filling patterns is far more restrained than before.

There is still an echo of contemporary woven silk design in these new patterns. Wavy bands of ornament and scattered flowers also figure on French silks of the 1760s.[2] However, the new airiness of design in lace also represented a reaction to the great popularity of lighter silk bobbin lace or blonde, which began in the 1750s. The trousseau of Wilhelmina Carolina of Orange (1743-1787), whose marriage to Karel Christiaan of Nassau-Wielburg (1743-1787) took place on 5 March 1760, included two sets of blonde lace, but there was also a set of Brussels lace comprising lappets, a pair of triple sleeve ruffles, a cape, a border, a collar and 'a pair of small sleeve ruffles for the shift'.[3] The princess also had a fan of Brussels lace mounted on ivory sticks, the lace for this costing ƒ52.10, the sticks and the mounting of the lace on them ƒ34.15.[4] Seven years later, in 1767, the trousseau of Wilhelmina of Prussia still included 'A set of a cap and triple sleeve ruffles and a jacket, Brussels lace, for the wedding Deshabillé', as well as numerous other Brussels lace items, although blonde was actually accorded a section of its own in the list.[5]

1. Risselin-Steenebrugen 1956, p. 218.
2. Rothstein 1990, pls. 284, 286.
3. Koninklijk Huisarchief, The Hague, 506-1-a.
4. Idem, A17 no. 516.
5. idem, A. 315-A-32.

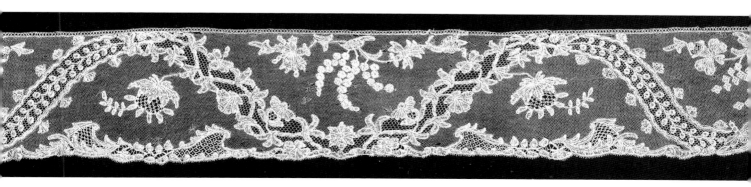

47
FLOUNCE, BRUSSELS BOBBIN LACE, SOUTHERN NETHERLANDS,
1765-1780

---

270 x 60 cm
Inv. no. BK-1975-359
Provenance: purchased from art-dealer Madame L. Collette-Payre, Paris, 1975;
donated by Het Kantsalet to mark its golden jubilee, 1975
Literature/Exhibition: Burgers 1990(2), cat. no. 8

This delicate lace clearly represents a later stage in lace design than the furnishing flounce cat. no. 44. The design principles are much the same, with the arrangement in a series of compartments, but the floral trails and wavy lines of linked ovals that separate the compartments horizontally are now much lighter and more playful than the earlier patterned scrolls, as are the swags above and the intertwined bands and flowers below. The flowers are quite naturalistic, with roses, carnations and tulips recognizable among them. An even more delicate basket of flowers appears in combination with a wavy line of linked ovals on a Benediction veil of Brussels bobbin lace dated 1770, which was formerly in Brussels Cathedral and is now in the Musées Royaux

d'Art et d'Histoire (fig. 47a). The development of floral design is reflected in a letter of 22 May 1766 from Jean-Baptiste Godfroy in Paris to Jean Du Rondeau in Brussels in respect of a recent consignment of lace, 'the design is too heavy, that is to say the flowers are not sufficiently separated...if you send some more, the bouquets must be prettier'.[1] The same lightness and prettiness can clearly be seen in the designs published by the painter and decorative artist Pierre Ranson (1736-1786) in Paris in 1776 in his various *Cahiers* (fig. 47b),[2] while the ribbon bows resemble some of those in the *Cahier de six noeuds de Rubans. Ornée de Fleurs, et Gravée en manière de deux Crayons* published in 1776 by the designer Jean-Baptist Pillement (1719-1809).

Naturally, the new tendency was also reflected in French lace design: light nosegays of flowers tied with ribbon bows almost as prominent as those on the Rijksmuseum lace, appear above similar intertwined ornament on the deep Argentan needle lace borders of a pair of albs in the Basilica of St Antony at Padua, which are said to have been presented to the saint's shrine by Marie Antoinette (1755-93) in the years after her marriage in 1770.[3]

A flounce identical to this one was exhibited in Paris in 1906. It belonged to the collection of a Madame de Poles.[4]

1. Risselin-Steenebrugen 1956, p. 218.
2. See, for example, Clouzot 1918, pl. 36 for a comparable swag of roses and groups of flowers and pl. 38 for swags of roses tied with ribbon bows. At least one of the designs is dated 1773. Ranson became director of the tapestry workshop at Aubusson in 1780.
3. Davanzo Poli 1995, no. 36, pl. XXXII.
4. Exposition, Paris 1906, pl. 1.

48

PAIR OF LAPPETS, VALENCIENNES BOBBIN LACE, FRANCE OR SOUTHERN NETHERLANDS, 1770-1780

9.5 x 5.25 cm
Inv. no. BK-NM-12633
Provenance: donated by H.C. Rehbock, 1920
Literature/Exhibition: Meulen-Nulle 1936, fig. 46

As patterns on lappets diminished and the ground became ever more prominent, Valenciennes lace underwent a change of technique. More threads were added to the solid parts of the design as they were worked to heighten the contrast between them and the ground. The design of these lappets exhibits a last vestige of the wavy bands that had been so prominent earlier in the century, while the flower sprigs have now become completely stylized and the border has been reduced to a minimum.

This new type of design is referred to by Claire Tribout of the leading firm in Valenciennes (see cat. no. 45) in a letter of 5 April 1771 to her contact in Brussels, in which she refers to a pair of sleeve ruffles 'of a new design and good taste, light, the flowers well caught and the mesh well made and solid'.[1] The marriage of the Dauphin and Marie Antoinette in Paris in 1770 led to a revival of the trade and numerous orders, Madame Tribout reporting that only Valenciennes was being worn everywhere, the consequence of this being that stocks ran low and prices became high.[2] After 1773, however, signs of a decline began to appear. By 1778 the number of workers, which had been 4,000 around 1760, had halved and it halved again by 1789. By 1788 there were

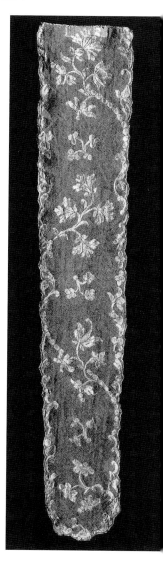

47a. Benediction veil, Brussels bobbin lace, Southern Netherlands, dated 1770. Musées Royaux d'Art et d'Histoire, Brussels. Inv. no. D. 4338

47b. Design by Pierre Ranson (1736-1786) from his Cahiers of 1776. (Reproduced from H. Clouzot, *Pierre Ranson. Peintre de Fleurs et d'Arabesques*, Paris 1918, pl. 36)

67

only four lace merchants left in Valenciennes and in December 1792 the Brussels correspondent of Claire Tribout, who had taken over the family firm in 1778, returned three pairs of ruffles, declaring that 'the sale of these articles is absolutely dead at this moment'. Finally, in 1795, Claire Tribout fled the country and her goods were seized and sold by the State.[3]

Valenciennes lace was noted for the whiteness of its clothwork, but these lappets are of a colour that reveals a further history in the late 19th century. The *Dictionary of Needlework* of 1882 notes that 'The right colour for old Lace is that of the unbleached thread', which can be achieved by laying it 'in the water in which coffee has been boiled', adding a recipe as follows: 'Take a quarter of a pound of the very best coffee, grind it at home, and pour six pints of boiling water upon it; let it remain for thirty minutes, and strain it through muslin'. Under 'Écru' in the same work we read, 'Much lace is sold of this colour, a hue which may be more fully described as *Café au lait*'. It was not age which gave many old laces a brownish tinge, but the dictates of late 19th-century fashion.

1. Maletot 1927, p. 30.
2. Ibid, p. 33.
3. Ibid., pp. 40, 43; Guignet 1979, p. 99.

49

LAPPET, ARGENTAN NEEDLE LACE, FRANCE, 1770-1775

---

57 x 10 cm
Inv. no. BK-1970-232
Provenance: collection of Mrs A. Jiskoot-Pierson, a former President of Het Kantsalet;
bequeathed to Het Kantsalet, 1970; donated by Het Kantsalet, 1970
Literature/Exhibition: Erkelens 1970, cat. no. 72

Playful designs like that of this lappet with its capricious wavy lines with little flower sprigs at intervals were to have a renewed appeal for lace designers towards the end of the 19th century, when the Louis XVI style was increasingly turned to for inspiration. Ribbons curling and winding in just such a way and interspersed with nosegays of flowers can be seen, for example as part of the much more extensive design on a veil of Brussels application lace, which was bought by Queen Emma from the Brussels firm Maison Sacré probably in 1896.[1]

Lace with a hexagonal mesh strengthened by buttonhole stitch (*brides bouclées*), as in this lappet, has traditionally been attributed to Argentan, but in fact it seems to have been made equally as much in neighbouring Alençon. In a report to the Provincial Assembly in 1787, it was stated that in 1772 sales of Argentan lace amounted to around 600,000 livres a year.[2] The report further noted, 'Point d'Argentan has always exhibited more beauty and perfection than that of Alençon, because the best quality only has always maintained *there'*. This may well have been because the lace with its strong mesh took longer to make than Alençon, but it may also have referred to the production of the Argentan workers in general, which included lace in the Alençon technique. It is interesting to note that Argentan is the only lace referred to by name among the extensive purchases made by Madame du Barry in the 1770s.[3]

1. Now on loan to the Centraal Museum, Utrecht, Inv. no. 23876. Wardle 1998, p. 41 and fig. 11.
2. Laprade 1905, p. 108.
3. Levey 1983, p. 53.

50
CAP, ALENÇON NEEDLE LACE, FRANCE, C. 1780

97 x 40 cm
Inv. no. BK-13253-A
Provenance: on loan from Mrs C.V. de Visser-Roelofs, 1925; donated by her, 1930
Literature/Exhibition: Oude Kant 1938, p. 15, no. 2;
Erkelens 1955, fig. 30; Wardle 1994, fig. 7

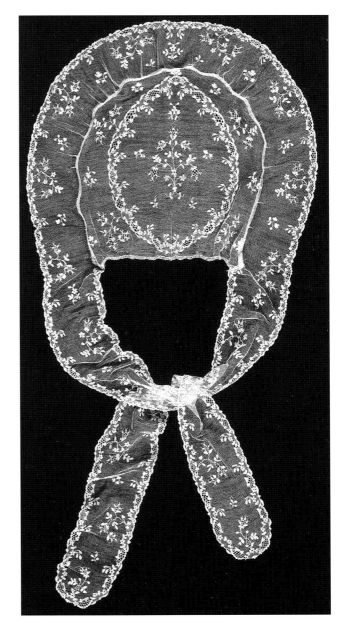

The lace of this cap is near the end of the development which saw the reduction of patterning to a border and a few scattered motifs, while the cap itself dates from the last period of this long-lived type of headgear. Lappets with a pattern nearly as light as that in this cap appear in a portrait of 1778 by Virgil Eriksen (1722-1782) of Queen Juliane Marie of Denmark (1773-1780), hanging down beside her face and falling over her shoulders.[1] With the advent of sober neo-classical fashions caps of this type disappeared from the scene. The lace industry was badly hit by the new mode. In a report to the Provincial Assembly in 1787 it was stated that, whereas in 1772 lace making at Alençon had occupied more than 10,000 workers (some of them as young as six years old), now it was much diminished and prices were falling, owing to the recent decline in demand, while gauze was in many cases being preferred to lace. This decline, it was pointed out, was common to almost all kinds of de luxe manufactures.[2] However, needle lace did continue to be worn at court, so that the industries at Alençon and Argentan managed to keep going, even though much reduced. Classical motifs were adopted in lace design too, but there is as yet no trace of them in the purely floral pattern here. In the 1770s and 1780s the names of five designers resident in Alençon are recorded in the archives there: Noël Paton, Louis Aubert, Julien-Noël Roger, Pierre-François Verdier and Jacques Sequret.[3] This suggests that the advent of simpler patterns made it less necessary to rely on designs brought in from Paris.

1. Levey 1983, fig. 344A.
2. Laprade 1905, p. 107.
3. Depierres 1886, p. 67, note 1.

57a. Jan Willem Pieneman (1779-1853), *Portrait of Agatha Petronella Hartsen (1814-1878), signed and dated 1841. Inv. no. A 4123*

1840s lace with designs that initiate the rococo revival that was soon to dominate lace design in a much bolder form. The cartouches along the lower edge of the veil were obviously inspired by 18th-century models, but the scrolling stems that curl up from them in a slanting movement represent a development of the delicately naturalistic vertical wavy flower trails found on some earlier bonnet veils.[1] The fashion for large bonnet veils began in the second half of the 1820s and continued through to the late 1840s.

Similarly delicately patterned lace was worn by Agatha Petronella Hartsen (1814-1878) for her wedding to Jan van der Hoop (1811-1897) on 17 March 1841 and as she sat for her portrait afterwards (fig. 57a).

1. Cf. Risselin-Steenebrugen 1980, figs. 334, 335.

This extremely delicate lace is described in Queen Wilhelmina's inventory as 'very costly' and it was doubtless for this reason that she lent it to various exhibitions. It is an excellent example of the refinement of some

58

MATCHING FLOUNCES, CHANTILLY BLACK SILK BOBBIN LACE, FRANCE, 1850-1855

750 x 27 cm, 485 x 13 cm
Inv. no. BK-BR-J-56-A-B
Provenance: inventory of Queen Emma, nos. 44a and b, gift from the King, Christmas 1881; on loan from the Koninklijke Verzamelingen, The Hague, 1966
Literature/Exhibition: Erkelens & Burgers, cat. no. 240; Levey 1983, fig. 419; Wardle & De Jong, 1985, cat. no. 42

58a. Flounce of Brussels needle lace, *point de gaze*, Belgium, Brussels, Maison Verdé-Delisle & Cie, c. 1867. Musées Royaux d'Art et d'Histoire, Brussels, Inv. D.3471

Black silk lace of fine quality was still being made at Chantilly itself up to the middle of the 19th century, which explains why this type of lace continued to bear that name even after production had been wholly taken over by the firms of Lefébure and Verdé-Delisle & Cie of Bayeux. In the 1840s the manufacturers had adopted the practice of making the lace in narrow strips, which were joined together by a stitch known as *point de raccroc*.[1] The lines of the joins can clearly be seen in places in these two matching flounces. However, as yet they show no signs of the shading achieved by the introduction, alongside the traditional half stitch, of whole stitch and a variety of fancy filling stitches, an innovation of the Second Empire period. It is quite possible that these flounces were actually made in Chantilly itself, in view of the remark in the Report of the Jury of the Great Exhibition of 1851 in London that the pieces made there were 'less intended for general use than to satisfy the desires of the luxurious, being laces of the very finest textures and most beautiful patterns'.[2]

The design here, composed entirely of flowers and large fernlike fronds anticipates later purely floral designs, such as that which featured in Verdé-Delisle & Cie's display in the Paris Exhibition of 1867, where three fern fronds are likewise prominent, but now as part of a design with a much more dynamic movement. The lace shown in 1867 was Chantilly lace, but the design was also used for Brussels *point de gaze* and application lace (fig. 58a).[3]

The great slump that hit the hand lace industry on the collapse of the Second Empire in 1871 left the manufacturers with huge stocks on their hands of what had previously been one of the prime fashion laces. This they were obliged to sell off as and when they could, which might explain how this piece came to be bought by William III in 1881 as a present for his young wife. At the International Exhibition of 1889 in Paris the manufacture of Chantilly lace was described as more of an art than an industry. By then it was produced solely for prestige purposes.

1. For good illustrations of the technique see Coppens 1984, ills. 13-16.
2. *Exhibition of the Works of Industry of All Nations* (London 1851). *Reports of the Juries*. IV (1852), p. 1021.
3. See Wardle & De Jong 1985, cat. no. 49 and Smolar-Meynart 1991, cat. no. 2, a piece said to have come from the collection of Empress Elisabeth of Austria (1837-1898), see Dreger 1906, p.19, fig.30.

59

HANDKERCHIEF, BOBBIN LACE, DENTELLE DE GAND,
VALENCIENNES TECHNIQUE, BELGIUM, GHENT, VISITATION
CONVENT, 1852-1867

41 x 42 cm
Inv. no. BK-1973-102
Provenance: collection of Mrs A. Pierson-Muysken,
a former President of Het Kantsalet; donated by her children, 1973
Literature/Exhibition: Risselin-Steenebrugen 1978, pp.151-152; Burgers 1990(2),
cat. no. 67

Lace-trimmed handkerchiefs returned to favour in the 1840s with the advent of dresses that looked back to the period around 1600, when such accessories had first become prominent. They remained in vogue for the rest of the 19th century. This example, however, is not just trimmed with lace, but entirely bobbin-made, the centre in particular being a real tour de force. It was one of the gems of the collection of its former owner and it represents the ultimate refinement of the Valenciennes technique achieved in the 19th century. Along with comparable handkerchiefs in New York and Brussels, it has been unhesitatingly attributed to the Convent of Nôtre Dame de la Visitation in Ghent.[1]

Lace in the Valenciennes technique was already being made at Ghent in the 18th century. Valenciennes lace production in general was badly hit by the French Revolution and its aftermath, but around 1833 the manufacturer Félix Duhaijon-Brunfaut of Ypres decided to revitalise the industry.[2] He brought in more up-to-date designs and employed the method of adding supplementary threads for the solidly-worked motifs, so as

to achieve a greater contrast with the airy square mesh ground. Later, between 1840 and 1850, further variety was introduced by the use of half-stitch, various fancy meshes, fond de neige in particular, and sometimes even needle-made ornaments. All this gave the lace a great boost and by 1851 Belgium had gained a virtual monopoly of its manufacture.[3]

A still more radical development took place in Ghent, where in 1852 Sister Marie-Joseph (Virginie Vrancken, d.1858), the Superior of the Visitation Convent, patented a lace to which she gave the name dentelle de Gand. The motifs still had the dense clothwork of traditional Valenciennes, but they were now made separately and the design was then assembled and the ground worked round it in the manner of Brussels bobbin lace. Already in 1853 the convent was able to present Arch-Duchess Marie-Henriette (1836-1902), on her marriage to Prince Leopold (the later King Leopold II, 1835-1909), with a dress in dentelle de Gand made at the École Saint-Joseph and the Filles Bleues Orphanage, which the convent also directed. After the death of Sister Marie-Joseph in 1858 the fortunes of the convent declined and in 1867 the production of lace ceased.

1. Risselin-Steenebrugen 1978, p.152.
2. Aubry 1854, p.72.
3. Idem, p.24.

60

FLOUNCE, ALENÇON LACE, FRANCE, 1860-1870

345 x 38 cm
Inv. no. BK-1966-91
Provenance: purchased from art-dealer Madame L. Collette-Payre, Paris, 1966
Literature/Exhibition: Burgers 1990(2), cat. no. 64

Costly though it was, Alençon needle lace became one of the leading fashion laces of the 19th century, thanks largely to the efforts of the two most important French firms of the day, Lefébure (later Lefébure Frères) and the Compagnie des Indes (also known after 1865 as Verdé-Delisle & Cie), both based in Paris. Auguste Lefébure already showed a scarf of Alençon lace at the Great Exhibition of 1851 in London and in the course of the 1850s he established control over a sizable proportion of the industry in the town. The Compagnie des Indes entered into a business agreement with the Alençon lace firm of Madame Besnard (née Couhier) in 1854 and in 1857 established a lace school under her direction at the Château de Lonrai. Both firms paid great attention to design and were among the few lace businesses of the day which could afford to have designers on their own staff. The names of those who worked for the

designed by Alcide Roussel, which was shown by Lefébure in the same exhibition[3] and which features a richly ornamented lace-like band looped in much the same exuberant way and with the same kind of 'gophering' as the ornament round the medallions here. This use of 'lace' as part of lace design, which can again be traced back to an 18th-century fashion (see cat. no. 38), was quite common in the late 1850s and 1860s. In the collection of designs from the Brussels firm of Patte-Hannot, now in the Musées Royaux d'Art et d'Histoire, there is another elaborate pattern of this kind from Paris, which is dated 10 October 1859 and signed *V[or] Le Clère dessinateur en dentelles*.

1. Wardle 1968, pp. 56-59, Minne-Dansaert 1905, p. 25.
2. Wardle 1968, fig. 1, p.58.
3. Ibid. pl. 14.

61

FLOUNCE, BRUSSELS BOBBIN AND NEEDLE LACE APPLIED TO MACHINE NET, BELGIUM, 1860-1870

240 x 36 cm
Inv. no. BK-1975-109
Provenance: purchased from art-dealer Madame L. Collette-Payre, Paris, 1973
Literature/Exhibition: Burgers 1990(2), cat. no. 71

Boldness of design and delicacy of execution are combined in this flounce,[1] which epitomises many of the aspects of Second Empire lace. The design was obviously inspired by 18th-century models (nos. 44, 47), but the wavy ribbon at the top has a freer character such as is already found in a similar ribbon in a Brussels application flounce shown by A. Delahaye at the Great Exhibition of 1851 in London.[2] The latter is, however, closer in spirit to the 18th-century models in that its formal ornament is also of rococo inspiration, whereas in the Rijksmuseum flounce the bold hoops over the ornamental band along the bottom exhibit an exuber-

Compagnie des Indes are not known, but from the 1850s until into the 20th century the leading designer for Lefébure was Alcide Roussel, who won the first of many medals at an exhibition in Brussels in 1856 and was still being praised for his 'unrivaled designs' in 1905.[1]

The extravagantly looped festoon of roses, anemones and forget-me-nots in this flounce is to some extent reminiscent of the entirely floral design of an Alençon flounce shown by Verdé-Delisle & Cie at the International Exhibition of 1867 in Paris.[2] The movement in the festoon is also close in spirit to a flounce

ance entirely of the 19th century. The ornament in the band and pendant from it and the sections of Greek key pattern echo the classical ornament increasingly found on silver and jewellery from the mid 1850s onwards. The flowers in the swags, posies and trails, among which can be recognized rose, convolvulus, tulip and heart's ease, have the appealing naturalism that characterizes much of the best lace of the second half of the 19th century.

1. See also Risselin-Steenebrugen 1980, p.466 and fig.336.
2. Wardle 1968, Fig.5 on p.106.

62

SHAWL, CHANTILLY BLACK SILK BOBBIN LACE, FRANCE, 1860-1870

---

287 x 148 cm
Inv. no. BK-1991-17
Provenance: given by Mr and Mrs van Haersma Buma-Six, 1991

As crinolines became ever wider in the Second Empire period, so the large shawls of Chantilly black silk bobbin lace or Brussels application lace that were worn with them were obliged to follow suit. This example is not among the largest, but it does exhibit the special refine-

in Paris in *The Englishwoman's Domestic Magazine* of June 1867 readers were informed that the lace shawls there 'are really splendid, and they are fashionable this year. In fact there is nothing more elegant than a shawl of black Chantilly lace over a dress of gros-grain silk or gaze de soie'[2]. Black silk lace was also produced in quantity at Grammont in Belgium, but the designs there were in general less refined.[3]

1. International Exhibition (London, 1862). *Repat of the Jury Class 24 Lace*, France, p.4.
2. *The English Woman's Domestic Magazine III* (1867), p. 313.
3. See Coppens 1984, ill. 21, figs. 4, 9, 10, 17, 23-26.

63

CHRISTENING ROBE, CAP, CUSHION AND VEIL, NEEDLE LACE, POINT DE GAZE, AND BRUSSELS BOBBIN LACE APPLIED TO MACHINE NET, BELGIUM, BRUSSELS, 1880

Height of robe 170 cm; width of cap 24 cm; cushion 60 x 36 cm; veil 90 x 118 cm
Inv. nos. BK-BR-J-388, 389, 383, 390
Provenance: purchased for the christening of Princess Wilhelmina in 1880; on loan from the Koninklijke Verzamelingen, The Hague, 1966
Literature/Exhibition: Erkelens & Burgers 1966, cat. nos. 107-110; Braam et al 1998, cat. no. 1

The exact provenance of this christening set is not recorded, but in the accounts of William III for 1880 there is a signed receipt from Léon Sacré for the large sum of 757 guilders and twenty cents, which may well relate to it.[1] Sacré, who had been making a name for himself all through the 1870s after taking over the family firm of Duchène-Pierron, figures as the leading supplier of fine lace to the Dutch royal family in surviving accounts from 1882 onwards.

The birth of a daughter, Wilhelmina Helena Pauline Maria (1880-1956), on 31 August 1880 to the elderly William III and his young second wife, Emma of Waldeck-Pyrmont, was an occasion for great rejoicing and the new princess appeared at her christening on 12 October in costly Brussels needle lace that was just as much ahead of fashion as that of her elder step-brother had been in 1840 (cat. no. 56). The front of the christening robe bears the royal arms in a conspicuous position in the widest part of the central panel, which is further patterned with bouquets, swags and festoons of flowers and delicate pendant leafy sprays in the style that was to typify lace design in the 1880s. All this is surrounded by a border of controlled foliate and floral scrolls, representing a considerable tightening of the more exuberant designs of the Second Empire period. Already present here are many of the elements of the revived rococo style that was to characterize much of 1880s design.

1. Koninklijk Huisarchief, The Hague, E.8.6.

fig. 62a. Two shawls, Brussels application lace, exhibited by Verde Delisle & Cie, Paris 1867. Reproduced from the *Art Journal 1867*

ment of an area along the top edge, which is meant to be turned down like a collar. The design and ornament are typical of shawl design of the 1860s with the pendant sprays of flowers, the prominent strap-work and foliate scrolls, the medallions with roses above and pendant leaves below and the heart motifs along the border between them. Similar elements can be recognized in two shawls of Brussels application lace shown at the International Exhibition of 1867 in Paris by Verdé-Delisle & Cie (fig. 62a).

In the Report of the Jury of Class 24, Lace, at the International Exhibition of 1862 in London, it was stated that 'The lace-girls of Caen, Bayeux and Chantilly...are very quick and celebrated for being the cleverest lace-workers in the world for black-lace shawls. There are 50,000 women regularly employed on this description of goods'[1], while in notes on the 'Great Exhibition' of 1867

68

COLLAR AND CUFFS, POLYCHROME SILK BOBBIN LACE, JESURUM
POLYCHROME LACE, ITALY, VENICE, M. JESURUM & CIE, 1896

---

140 x 13, 24 x 7.5 cm
Inv. no. BK-BR-J-304
Provenance: purchased by Queen Emma in Venice, 1896; inventory of Queen Wilhelmina:
Guipure I; on loan from the Koninklijke Verzamelingen, The Hague, 1966
Literature/Exhibition: Erkelens & Burgers 1966, cat. no. 277;
Wardle & De Jong 1985, cat. no. 159; Wardle 1998, p. 45

Queen Mother Emma bought this set from the Jesurum firm during a visit to Venice in November 1896, probably as a present for Wilhelmina who went with her.[1] Michelangelo Jesurum (1844-1909), who founded his lace company in 1870, stated that he himself invented this polychrome lace in 1877. Already awarded a gold medal at the International Exhibition in Paris in 1878, it epitomizes the sort of de luxe item introduced by various manufacturers in the last quarter of the 19th century in the hope that it would be difficult for the machine lace manufacturers to imitate. The technique of the polychrome lace resembles that of Belgian *Duchesse* lace and many of its design features are of similar derivation. This set with its charming pastel colours against a ground of green bars, incorporates elements typical of 1890s lace design, such as the elongated C-scrolls and the fanlike forms at the sides, motifs also found in a fan leaf design of around the turn of the century in which the formal element predominates over the flowers.[2] The set undoubtedly represents the finest quality of this type of lace,[3] the manufacture of which seems to have been concentrated on the lace school opened by Jesurum in 1878 at the firm's headquarters on Ponte Canonica in the parish of San Zaccaria in Venice. It is even possible that Queen Mother Emma saw lace of this type being made during her visit to Jesurum's shop. Although this lace was evidently imitated by at least one other firm in Venice, Jesurum remained the leading producer.[4]

1. It heads the bill from Jesurum, Koninklijk Huisarchief, The Hague, A 47A III 45, but does not appear in Queen Emma's inventory.
2. Carlier de Lantsheer, n.d. (c. 1905), pl. 82.
3. Cf. Mariarcher et al 1986, figs. 11-26, 28-30, 32-34.
4. Ibid., pp. 106-109, 140-141.

69

PARASOL, NEEDLE LACE, POINT DE GAZE, WITH SOME BOBBIN LACE,
BELGIUM, BRUSSELS, MAISON SACRÉ, 1897

Lace: diam. 51 cm; parasol: h. 90 cm
Inv. no. BK-BR-J-17
Provenance: delivered to Queen Emma, 1898; collection of Queen Wilhelmina; on loan
from the Koninklijke Verzamelingen, The Hague, 1966
Literature: Carlier de Lantsheer, n.d. [c.1905], pl.67; Erkelens & Burgers 1966,
cat. no 99; Wardle 1998, pp. 40-41

The lace here must be the '*Parasol cover extra fine needlepoint*', which figures in Léon Sacré's bill to Queen Emma of 12 December 1898.[1] It cost 2,500 francs. The design is typical of the 1890s in its lively, capricious scrollwork round the bouquets of flowers, which makes an almost flame-like effect in places. The parasol was obviously a prestigious piece and as such was chosen by Carlier de Lantsheere for inclusion in his book of c. 1905 extolling the hand lace industry.[2] Most of the other Sacré *point de gaze* pieces illustrated there are, however, much more static in design and the beginnings of this change can already be seen in the more sober scrolls and cartouches in the central part of the parasol.

The fine lace was given quite an elaborate mount made by Dupuy of 8 Rue de la Paix in Paris, with a gold handle,

tip and knobs at the ends of the ribs set with pastes. The parasol was ordered as a Christmas present for Queen Wilhelmina in 1897. She is carrying it in an undated photograph showing her with her husband probably around 1901 (fig. 69a). Queen Mother Emma also bought a 'bertha' collar and flounce of matching design from Sacré, which were given to Wilhelmina on her birthday in August 1900.[3]

The superb quality of this lace entirely illustrates the contention of an anonymous writer in the *Connoisseur* of June 1905,[4] who considered 'Real Lace a Good Investment': 'Among the modern real laces of today which are really worth collecting, there is none which is a better investment than fine Brussels Point - "The Queen of Lace". This lovely article, made entirely with the needle of the finest linen thread [much of it is actually made of cotton], is getting scarcer each year, and in the course of another fifteen or twenty years will find its place among the many other beautiful specimens of "Needle Point" work not to be had today'. These prophetic words were to prove all too true.

1. Koninklijk Huisarchief, The Hague, A 47a.III.46.
2. Carlier de Lantsheer n.d. (c. 1905), pl. 67. See pls. 118-120 for the other point de gaze pieces.
3. Erkelens & Burgers, cat. nos. 100, 101 (the references in Queen Emma's inventory suggested there may be incorrect); see Braam et al 1998, p. 31: Sacré sent a bill for all three pieces to Wilhelmina by mistake.
4. (June 1905), p.116.

69a. Queen Wilhelmina and Prince Hendrik (1876-1934), postcard

with photograph by Ebner, The Hague, probably 1901

70

COLLAR, BOBBIN AND NEEDLE LACE ON NEEDLE-MADE GROUND,
POINT D'ANGLETERRE, BELGIUM, c. 1900

Width 15 cm
Inv. no. BK-1985-100
Provenance: donated by Het Kantsalet, 1985

This type of collar is longer and has more fulness than the earlier 'bertha'. It came into vogue in the 1890s. It was known as a *godet* and was intended to be worn fairly flat with the superfluous lace draped in various ways so that it was vaguely reminiscent of an inverted pleat, the more normal meaning of the term *godet*.

The lace is of a new type evolved in the second half of the 19th century, in which bobbin and needle-made motifs are set on the needle-made ground used for *point de gaze*. This lace, which was made only in Belgium, was given the old name *point d'Angleterre*. One of the firms that made a speciality of it was Minne-Dansaert, originally in Brussels, but after 1889 at Haeltert where by then it had most of its workers. A collar of the same design appears as no. 10905 in a sales catalogue of c. 1903 of the lace merchant and manufacturer Louis Franke (1872-1950) of Wiesbaden and Brussels, who doubtless obtained it from one of his numerous suppliers in Belgium.[1] It may even have come from the convent at Liedekerke in Brabant, which was renowned for its beautiful Brussels application lace and *point d'Angleterre*, and which figures on a long list of the firm's contacts.[2] That the collar still appears in Franke's catalogue of 1910 illustrates the longevity of a popular design, such as this undoubtedly was.[3]

While *point d'Angleterre* can sometimes be highly contem-porary in design[4] and the flowers here are characteristic of the lighter laces of the period around 1900-1914, the patterns used for it often look back to the 18th century with elements like the fancy fillings to be found here in the linked rococo-style cartouches along the lower edge. These clearly illustrate remarks made by the lace manufacturer Ernest Lefébure in 1900 regarding the decades after the slump of 1870, 'Never before was so much effort made to discover the construction of ancient stitches, the tradition of which was lost. In France, Belgium and Austria, much effort has been devoted to renewing the designs and finding fresh decorative effects, in which the utmost advantage could be taken of the technical resources, thus establishing the making of hand-made lace as an art-industry, worthy of appearing in Museums, and in the Annual Exhibitions'.[5]

1. See article by L. Immenroth in Framke 1995.
2. Verhaegen 1902, vol.I, pp. 148, 204-206, 223.
3. For other examples see Mottola Molfino 1984, p. 291, cat. 359; Coppens 1981, cat. 57; Smolar-Meynaert & Vincke 1982, cat. no. 51; Bruggeman 1997, p. 74; Feligioni, n.d. (1997), p.30. There is also a bertha collar of this design in the possession of the Queen of Norway; information kindly supplied by Toos de Klerk.
4. Levey 1983, figs. 435, 453.
5. Lefébure 1912, pp. 94-97.

71

DRESS, TAPE LACE WITH NEEDLE-MADE FILLINGS AND MACHINE-MADE INSERTIONS AND EDGINGS, PROBABLY BELGIUM, 1900-1910

Length at front 149 cm, at back 194 cm
Inv. no. BK-2000-2
Provenance: collection of a family in The Hague;
donated by Het Kantsalet to mark its 75th anniversary, 2000

It would be difficult to imagine a greater contrast than that between the parasol of 1898 (cat. no. 69) or the contemporary *godet* (cat. no. 70) and this tape lace dress. This extreme dichotomy is, however, characteristic of the last boom period of hand-made lace, when, in order to meet the constantly increasing competition from machine lace, manufacturers opted either for an ever greater refinement of technique or for work that could be turned out as rapidly as the machine product. The lace of this dress, a type variously known as *Luxeuil* or *point lacet*, among other names, obviously belongs to the second category. Nonetheless, it has its own subtlety. The symmetrical pattern of large flowers, leaves and C-scrolls is done in a plain and a patterned tape and also incorporates small leaf-shaped tapes. The tapes are joined together by a variety of wheel motifs, herringbone or faggot stitching and filling patterns. There are insertions of small roundels and panels of machine-embroidered net, which must have come from Plauen in Germany or St. Gallen in Switzerland, the principle centres for this work. The inset panels feature roses with petals that appear to be raised in the manner of Brussels, *point de gaze*. Finally, the sleeves are edged with narrow borders of machine-made Valenciennes lace from Calais in France or Nottingham in England.

Crude though the technique may be, dresses like this undoubtedly made a bold and striking effect when vie-wed from a distance. In this they vied with the bold, so-called Irish crochet that was also highly fashionable at the same period.

72

COLLAR, DUCHESSE BOBBIN LACE WITH MACHINE NET, NETHERLANDS, APELDOORN, DE NEDERLANDSCHE KANTWERKSCHOOL, 1903-1904, THE DESIGN: VIENNA, ZENTRAL SPITZENKURS, FRANZISKA HOFMANNINGER, 1901

---

54 x 20 cm
Inv. no. BK-BR-J-165
Provenance: purchased by Queen Emma from De Nederlandsche Kantwerkschool, Apeldoorn, 1904, inventory of Queen Emma, no. 83; on loan from the Koninklijke Verzamelingen, The Hague, 1966
Literature/Exhibition: Erkelens & Burgers, cat. no. 278; Levey 1983, fig. 494, Davanzo Poli 1984, p.292; Wardle & De Jong 1985, cat. no. 167; Wardle 1992, cat. no. 10; Wardle 1998, pp. 51-54

In the 1926 inventory of Queen Emma's lace this piece is described as 'bobbin-lace collar, modern design, bought in Apeldoorn at the lace school. Matching handkerchief'.[1] The collar was made in the Duchesse techique by Mien van der Meulen, who had joined the school as a teacher in 1903 and was to become its director on its move to The Hague in 1906. A trial-piece for the collar is now in the Museum Boijmans Van Beuningen in Rotterdam.[2] The design is an interpretation of one made at the Zentral Spitzenkurs in Vienna in 1901 by Franziska Hofmanninger (b. 1870).[3] It was obtained for

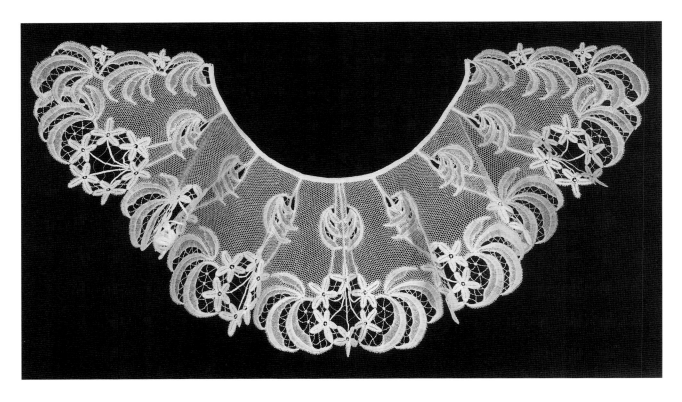

van Kunstnijverheid in Haarlem, of which he was director. The Apeldoorn version is on a larger scale than a collar made to the same design in Vienna in 1903 (fig. 72a) and the design has been interpreted somewhat differently, but in this bold rendering the Art Nouveau character comes out very clearly. While the plants and flowers in the superb designs made for needle lace at the Zentral Spitzenkurs are generally still quite clearly recognizable, those in the bobbin lace designs tend to show a higher degree of stylization, as is the case here. The technique, in which use is made of net as well as bars for the background, is also derived from the Viennese examples.

1. An earlier inventory has 'bought at a bazaar in The Hague, Lace School, Apeldoorn'. The handkerchief (border only), Erkelens & Burgers 1966, cat. no. 279.
2. Inv. no. 289c, Wardle 1992(1), cat. no. 11.
3. See Framke 1995, p.58.

72a. Collar, bobbin lace, designed by Franziska Hofmanninger, 1901, made at the Zentral Spitzen kurs, Vienna, 1903. Österreichisches Museum für Angewandte Kunst, Vienna

the Apeldoorn school at the International Exhibition of 1902 in Turin either by the school's first director, Agatha Wegerif-Gravestein (1867-1944), or, more probably, by its secretary-treasurer, Eduard von Saher, who was a member of the jury at the exhibition and is known to have made important purchases there for the Museum

73
COLLAR, NEEDLE LACE, DESIGNED AND MADE BY IRÈNE D'OLSZOWSKA, BELGIUM, BRUSSELS, c. 1905

---

125 x 18 cm
Inv. no. BK-BR-364
Provenance: probably purchased from the exhibition La Femme Belge, Kunstnijverheid Museum, Haarlem, 1914; on loan from the Nederlandsche Maatschappij voor Nijverheid en Handel, Haarlem, 1934
Literature/Exhibition: Wardle & De Jong 1985, cat. no. 167

As in Vienna, so too in Belgium Art Nouveau design in lace was initiated not by lace manufacturers, but by designers trained at art schools. Irène d'Olszowska studied design at the École Bischoffsheim in Brussels under the painter Adolphe Crespin (1859-1944), who himself made some lace designs.[1] In 1905 she was awarded a silver medal for lace design at the International Exhibition at Liège and by the time of the Brussels International Exhibition of 1910 she had made a name for herself. A larger version of this collar shown there was enthusiastically described as 'a veritable miracle'.[2] The design as a whole makes an obvious Art Nouveau effect, particularly in respect of the peacocks and the flowers in the inner border and such oriental elements as the key pattern and the play of lines between the peacocks and around the wreaths. However, certain elements, notably the flower garland and the circular wreath, turn up again in very similar forms in another lace collar designed by D'Olszowska in a purely neo-Louis XVI style.[3] D'Olszowska further made little or no distinction between lace designs and those for other techniques. Very similar peacocks again appear flanking floral roundels in a printed textile design exhibited in 1910, while a group of swallows in a needle lace fan recur in a batik table cloth.[4] Irène d'Olszowska enjoyed considerable renown in her day. She exhibited in association with the society Les Arts de la Femme and attracted commissions like that given by Queen Elisabeth of the Belgians (1876-1965) for a scarf in Mechlin bobbin lace after a prize-winning design.[5] Later on she was invited to make designs by the National Association for the Organization of Handmade Lace in England, a selection of these being exhibited in 1913 at the Mansion House in London.[6] In 1914 lace by her featured prominently in the exhibition *La Femme Belge* in Haarlem.[7] In 1909 it had been confidently predicted that she would 'found a school of lace design',[8] but the First World War put an end to these hopes.

1. Coppens 1982, p. 227.
2. Poupeye 1910, pp. 346-348. I am indebted to Toos de Klerk for this reference and that in note 3.
3. Stickerei-Zeitung, XII (1912), p. 290.
4. Coppens 1981, p. 119, cat. 83.
5. Khnopff 1912, pp. 325-326.
6. Mansion House 1913, pp. 4, 6, 7, 21.
7. Rogge 1914, pp. 392, 394, fig.6.
8. 'La Renaissance dentellière', Le Soir, 23 April 1909, no. 114. I am indebted to Marguerite Coppens for this reference.

74

COLLAR, DUCHESSE BOBBIN LACE, DESIGNED AND MADE BY
JOHANNA HENRIETTE FABER (1893-1962), NETHERLANDS,
AMSTERDAM, RIJKSSCHOOL VOOR KUNSTNIJVERHEID, c. 1915

---

49 x 22.5 cm
Inv. no. BK-1979-31
Provenance: donated to Het Kantsalet in 1979 by the maker's daughter, Miss A. Pleging; donated by Het Kantsalet, 1979
Literature/Exhibition: Wardle & De Jong 1985, cat. no. 175. Wardle 1992, cat. no. 47

Among all the lace discussed here, this is probably the only item that can be called a masterpiece in the original meaning of the word. The names of the students at the Rijksschool voor Kunstnijverheid (National Applied Art School), which was officially founded in 1882 and attached to the Rijksmuseum, are not recorded, but it is highly probable that Johanna Henriette Faber took the bobbin lace course there. This had been instituted by Mien van der Meulen-Nulle, who became a teacher at the school in 1911. In the second year of the two-year course *Duchesse* lace occupied a prominent position, students being required to make a piece with 'simple motifs and mesh ground' and a large item 'with free motifs and various fancy meshes'.[1] This collar certainly answers the second description and the fact that it was framed when presented to the Rijksmuseum indicates that it was the maker's masterpiece for her diploma. It is very well made and does indeed exhibit various fancy grounds. The shape is characteristic of the period 1910-1920, while the various motifs are typical of *Duchesse* lace at this period and the design as a whole is reminiscent of the coiling stem patterns of the 17th century. A handkerchief corner in the same technique made around 1914 by another student at the Rijksschool has a similar coiling stem design.[2]

In essence these designs hark back to those of Flemish bobbin lace and Venetian needle lace of the middle and second half of the 17th century. This eclectic tendency is further illustrated by another collar made by Henriette Faber to her own design in 1914-1916, which is a bobbin lace version of a geometrical *reticella* pattern.[3] It is no coincidence that the period around the turn of the century saw the publication of numerous examples of old lace, which were meant to inspire new designs. In 1904, for instance, Henri Lemaire, a designer of machine lace, published a vast selection of samples of real lace, which were intended 'to regenerate and renew the fashions of past centuries with the aid of motifs more in tune with the taste of our epoque'.[4]

In 1915 Henriette Faber succeeded Mien van der Meulen at the Rijksschool, remaining there until 1919. She retained her interest in lace making, publishing a course in the magazine *Het Blijde Huis* between 1930 and 1932.

1. Wardle 1992, pp. 102-103.
2. Ibid., cat. 44e.
3. Ibid. cat. 46. For commercial versions of similar designs made in Belgium and France see Carlier de Lantsheere, n.d. (c. 1905), pls. 3, 5-7, 88.
4. Lemaire 1904, title page.

75

SCARF WITH THE CROWNED CYPHER OF QUEEN WILHELMINA AND THE ROYAL ARMS OF THE NETHERLANDS, NEEDLE LACE, POINT DE VENISE, BELGIUM, FRANSCISCAN CONVENT, OPBRAKEL, SIGNED I. DE RUDDER, 1918

245 x 45 cm
Inv. no. BK-BR-J-233
Provenance: presented to Queen Wilhelmina in 1918 by the Committee of Belgian Refugees in gratitude for the shelter offered them in the Netherlands during the First World War; on loan from the Koninklijke Verzamelingen, The Hague, 1966
Literature/Exhibition: Kellogg 1920, pp. 207-209; Erkelens & Burgers 1966, cat. no. 123, Wardle 1989, pp.73-6, 79-86

This is one of the most prestigious items produced under the War Lace scheme which, under the auspices of the Comité de la Dentelle in Belgium and the Commission for Relief in Belgium in the United States, supplied materials and designs to lace makers in Belgium during the First World War in order to help them make a living.[1] The scarf was made at the Franciscan Convent at Opbrakel near Grammont, which had the reputation of being one of the finest centres in Belgium for the production of needle lace. Indeed, it was described as 'unquestionably first in Belgium in the production of figures in Point de Venise' by Charlotte Kellogg of the American Commission, who saw the scarf being made there in 1918.[2] Hence it was the obvious place to choose for the execution of this design, which incorporates a lively array of figures and had been specially made by the Belgian sculptor Isidore de Rudder (1855-1943). De Rudder, who, as one of the first artists commissioned to produce designs for War Lace, had made some innovative patterns featuring marine plants and animals,[3] adopted a rather more restrained manner for this scarf, which was probably intended as a table decoration rather than for wear. The central pattern of tulips and hyacinths, representing 'Dutch national flowers',[4] still has a distinctly Art Nouveau flavour, but the border of lilies-of-the-valley, 'symbolizing the return of happiness', and the elaborate compositions at the ends of the scarf are much more traditional in character. The latter are centred on the royal arms and motto wreathed with oak and surrounded by 'the children of Holland showering flowers of abundance upon the martyred children of their sister kingdom,' represented by the arms of the Belgian provinces below. The children, reminiscent of De Rudder's favourite putti, are surrounded by oranges, while the crowned monogram of Queen Wilhelmina appears in the scalloped border along with the dates of the First World War. The design, which is wholly typical of De Rudder's sculpture in its eclecticism, is worked in an impeccable technique, which demonstrates what the best lace makers in Belgium were capable of in the declining years of their industry.

1. Coppens 1990, pp. 116-122. ▶
2. Kellogg 1920, p. 209.
3. Wardle 1989, figs. 7-10; Coppens 1990, fig. 70.
4. Kellogg 1920, p. 207, where the symbolism is explained.

Bibliography

Adriaans 1992-3
H. Adriaans, 'Koninklijk Kant in het Centraal Museum, Utrecht', *Kostuum* 1992-3, pp. 20-25

Anciennes dentelles 1889
Anciennes dentelles belges formant la collection de feue Madame Augusta, Bnne Leids, et donné au Musée de Gruuthuus à Bruges, Antwerp 1889

Aubry 1854
F. Aubry, *Exposition universelle de Londres 1851 - Dentelles, Blondes, Tulles et Broderies*, Paris 1854

Besselièvre 1913
La Collection Besselièvre. Dentelles et Broderies anciennes, Paris 1913

Braam et al 1998
E. van Braam et al, *In Royal Array. Queen Wilhelmina 1880-1962. Koninklijk Gekleed. Koningin Wilhelmina 1880-1962*, Apeldoorn (Stichting Paleis Het Loo Natinaal Museum), Zwolle 1998

Bruggeman 1985
M. Bruggeman, *Brugge en Kant*, Bruges 1985

Bruggeman 1997
M. Bruggeman, *L'Europe de la Dentelle*, Bruges 1997

Buffevant 1984
B. de Buffevant, *L'Économie dentellière en région parisienne au XVIIe siècle*, Société historique et archéologique de Pontoise, du Val d'Oise et du Vexin, Pontoise 1984

Burgers 1990(1)
C.A. Burgers, 'Nederlandse Heraldiek uit de textiel verzameling van het Rijksmuseum. Kanttekeningen bij een kleine expositie', *Bulletin van het Rijksmuseum* 38 (1990), pp. 48-68

Burgers 1990(2)
C.A. Burgers, *40 jaar kant. Keuze van aanwinsten uit de jaren 1946-1986/40 years of lace. Selection of acquisitions over the years 1946-1986*, Rijksmuseum leaflet 1, 1990

Burgers 1992
C.A. Burgers, *Selection from the gift of textiles from Twickel and Weldam*, Rijksmuseum leaflet 4, 1992

Carlier de Lantsheere n.d. [c. 1905]
A. Carlier de Lantsheere, A., *Les Dentelles à la Main*, Brussels n.d. [c. 1905]

Carlier de Lantsheere 1922
A. Carlier de Lantsheer, A., *Trésor de l'art dentellier*, Brussels 1922

Carmigiani & Fossi Todorow 1981
M. Carmigiani & M. Fossi Todorow, *Dentelle a Palazzo Davanzati. Manufatture europee dal XVI al XX secolo*, Florence 1981

Catalogus Leeuwarden 1922
Exhib. cat. *Catalogus van de Kant-Tentoonstelling te Leeuwarden*, Leeuwarden (Fries-Museum) 1922

Cavallo 1966
A. Cavallo, *Textiles. Isabella Stewart Gardner Museum*, Boston 1966

Clouzot 1918
H. Clouzot, *Pierre Ranson. Peintre de fleurs et d'arabesques*, Paris 1918

Coppens 1981
M. Coppens, exhib. cat. *Kant uit België van de zestiende eeuw tot heden*, Brussels, Musées Royaux d'Art et d'Histoire, 1981

Coppens 1982
M. Coppens, 'La stylistique dentellière à l'époque Art Nouveau. Son évolution jusqu'a la première guerre mondiale', *Revue des Archéologues et Historiens d'Art de Louvain* (1982), pp.218-248

Coppens 1984
M. Coppens, *Gerardsbergen Chantillykant*, Gerardsbergen 1984

Coppens 1985
M. Coppens, 'Les Amis de la dentelle. Un mécénat de type pédagogique', in *Liber Memorialis 1935-1985*, Musées Royaux d'Art et d'Histoire, Brussels 1985, pp.271-281

Coppens 1990
M. Coppens, exhib. cat. *Les Dentelles Royales/Kant uit Koningshuis*, Brussels 1990

Coppens 1995(1)
M. Coppens, 'Les commandes dentellières de l'Union Patriotique des Femmes Belges et du Comité de la

Dentelle à Fernand Khnopff', *Revue Belge d'Archéologie et d'Histoire d'Art* LXIV (1995), pp. 71-83

Coppens 1995(2)
M. Coppens, 1995(2), 'Du "ballotin" à la mini réserve ambulante: de l'art d'emballer les dentelles au passé et au présent', *La vie des musées* 10 (1995), pp.15-22

Coppens 1996
M. Coppens, 'La dentelle de Binche dans la seconde moitié du XVIIIᵉ siècle: certitudes et questions', *Cahiers de Mariemont* 24-25 (1996), pp.126-137

Cox 1908
R. Cox, 'La Collection de M. Alfred Lescure', *Les Arts* 78 (1908), pp. 17-32

Dacier & Vuaflart
E. Dacier & A. Vuaflart, *Jean de Jullienne et les graveurs de Watteau au XVIIIᵉ siècle*, Paris 1929

Davanzo Poli 1984
D. Davanzo Poli (ed.), exhib. cat. *Cinque secoli di merletti europei. I Capolavori*, Burano 1984

Davanzo Poli 1991
D. Davanzo Poli, *Tessuti Antichi. La collezioni dei Musei Civici Veneziana*, Venice 1991

Davanzo Poli 1995
D. Davanzo Poli, *Basilica del Santo. I Tessuti*, Padua/Rome 1995

Davanzo Poli 1998
D. Davanzo Poli, *Il Merletto Veneziano*, Novara 1998

Despierres 1886
G. Despierres, *Histoire du point d'Alençon dépuis son origine jusqu'à nos jours*, Paris 1886

Dillen 1929-74
J.G. van Dillen, *Bronnen tot de geschiedenis van het bedrijfsleven en het gildewezen van Amsterdam*, 3 vols., The Hague 1929-74

Dreger 1906
M. Dreger, *De Wiener Spitzenaustellung 1906*, Leipzig 1906

Dreger 1910
M. Dreger, *Entwicklungsgeschichte der Spitze*, Vienna 1910

Erkelens 1955
A.M.L.E. Erkelens, *Kant/Laces*, Facetten uit de verzameling no. 5, Rijksmuseum Amsterdam 1955

Erkelens 1965
A.M.L.E. Erkelens, exhib. cat. *40 Jaar Kantsalet*, Het Kantsalet 1965

Erkelens & Burgers 1966
A.M.L.E. Erkelens & C.A. Burgers, exhib. cat. *Kant uit Koninklijk Bezit*, Rijksmuseum Amsterdam 1966

Erkelens 1970
A.M.L.E. Erkelens, exhib. cat. *De kantverzameling Jiskoot-Pierson. Een groot geschenk*, Rijksmuseum 1970

Exposition de Bruxelles 1910
Exhib. cat. *1910. Dentelles Broderies Classe 84*

Exposition Paris 1906
Exhib. cat. *Exposition de l'Union Centrale des Arts Décoratifs. 1906. Les Grandes Collections de Dentelles Anciennes et Modernes Exposées au Pavillion de Marsan*, Paris 1906

Exhib. cat. Paris 1983
Exhib. cat. *Modes en Dentelles 1590-1983*, Paris (Musée de la Mode et du Costume)1983

Feligoni n.d. [1997]
R. Feligioni, *Vanità e seduzione. Il merletto negli accessori di moda dell'Ottocento*, Centro Arnaldo Caprai, Foligno, n.d. [1997]

Fleming & Honour 1989
J. Fleming & H. Honour, *The Penguin Dictionary of Decorative Arts*, Harmondsworth 1989 (1st ed. 1977)

Framke 1995
G. Framke (ed.), *Spitze Luxus zwischen Tradition und Avantgarde*, Dortmund (Museum für Kunst und Kultuurgeschiedenis) 1995

Gächter-Weber 1997
M.Gächter-Weber, exhib. cat. *Spitzen umschreiben Gesichter*, Textilmuseum St Gallen, 1997

Graff-Höfgen 1976
G.Graff-Höfgen, 'Spitzen van Iklé und Jacoby', *Hamburgische Geschichts- und Heimatblätt*, Band 9 Heft 11, October 1976, pp.274-281

Graze 1997
D.Graze (ed.), *Dictionary of Women Artists*, London/Chicago 1997

Grieten & Bungeneers 1996
S.Grieten & J. Bungeneers (ed.), *Inventaris van het Kunstpatrimonium van de Provincie Antwerpen. De Onze-Lieve-Vrouwe Cathedral van Antwerpen*,vol. 3, Antwerp 1996

Gruber 1984
A. Gruber, *Chinoiserie. Der Einfluss Chinas auf die europäische Kunst 17.-19. Jahrhundert/L'influence de la Chine sur les arts en Europe XVIIe-XIXe siècle*, Abegg-Stiftung, Riggisberg 1984

Gruber 1985
A. Gruber, *Grotesken. Ein Ornamentstil in Textilien in des 16.-19. Jahrjunderts/Grotesques. Un style ornemental dans les arts textiles du XVIe-XIXe siècle*, Abegg-Stiftung, Riggisberg 1985

Guignet 1979
P. Guignet, 'The Lacemakers of Valenciennes in the Eighteenth Century', *Textile History* 10 (1979), pp.96-113

Hartkamp-Jonxis 1987
E. Hartkamp-Jonxis et al. (ed.), *Sits, oost-west relaties in textiel*, Zwolle, 1987

Haverkorn Van Rijsewijk 1905
P. Haverkorn Van Rijsewijk, 'Maria Strick', *Oud Holland* 23 (1905), pp. 52-62

Henneberg 1930
H. von Henneberg, *Stil und Technik der alten Spitzen*, Berlin 1930

Henstra 1992
D.J. Henstra, 'Kantnijverheid te Leeuwarden in de 17de en 18de eeuw', *De Vrije Fries* LXXII (1992), pp. 75-85

Het Hollandsch Interieur
Exhib. cat. *Het Hollandsch Interieur in de XVIIIe Eeuw* Rijksmuseum Amsterdam 1931

Histoire 1843
Histoire de la dentelle par M. de...., Paris 1843

Hudig 1943
C.J. Hudig, 'Kant en haar gebruik', *Historia* 8 (1943), pp.44-46

Iklé & Fäh n.d.
L. Iklé & A. Fäh, *Die Sammlung Iklé*, Zürich, n.d.

Irwin & Brett 1970
J. Irwin & K.B. Brett, *Origins of Chintz*, London 1970

Jackman 1990
S.W. Jackman, *Chére Annette*, Baarn 1990

Jarry 1981
M. Jarry, *Chinoiserie*, Fribourg 1981

Jong & Groot 1988
M. de Jong & I. de Groot, *Ornamentprenten in het Rijksprentenkabinet I. 15de & 16de Eeuw*, Rijksmuseum Amsterdam 1988

Jonge 1941
C.H. de Jonge, *Een eeuw Nederlandsche mode*, The Hague 1941

Kant n.d. [1961]
Kant, Boymans-van Beuningen Museum, Rotterdam n.d. [1961]

Kasteele n.d.
A.A. van de Kasteele, *Korte Handleiding tot de bezichtiging van het kabinet van zeldzaamheden*, The Hague n.d.

Kellen 1876
D. van der Kellen Jr, *Catalogus van het Museum van het Koninklijke Oudheidgenooschap*, Amsterdam 1876

Kellen 1879
D. van der Kellen Jr, 'De Relikwieën van het Huis van Oranje in der Nederlandsch Museum', *Nederlandsche Kunstbode* 1879, pp.3-5

Kellen n.d.
D. van der Kellen Jr, *Gids voor de bezoekers van het Nederlandsch Museum voor Geschiedenis en Kunst*, Amsterdam n.d.

Kellogg 1920
C. Kellogg, *Bobbins of Belgium*, New York/London 1920

Khnopff 1912
F. Khnopff, 'Studio Talk', *The Studio* LVI (1912), pp.325-326

Kinderen-Besier 1950
J.H. der Kinderen-Besier, *Spelevaert der Mode. De Kledij
onze Voorouders in de zeventiende eeuw*, Amsterdam 1950

Kist 1995
B. Kist, '"Alle klederen, dewelke dezen vorst aanhad-
de." Relikwieën van het Huis van Oranje in de histori-
sche afdeling van her Rijksmuseum', *Kostuumverzamelingen in beweging*, Nederlandse
Kostuumvereniging voor Mode en Streekdracht,
Arnhem 1995, pp. 33-42

Kraatz 1983
A. Kraatz (ed.), *Dentelles au Musée Historique des Tissus*,
Lyon 1983

Kraatz 1984
A. Kraatz, 'The Inventory of a Venetian Lace Merchant
dated 1671', *Bulletin de liaison du CIETA* 55-6 (1984), pp.
127-133

Kraatz 1992
A. Kraatz, *Les dentelles*, Musée national de la
Renaissance Château d'Ecouen, Paris 1992

Kunstzaal Kleykamp 1912
Exhib. cat. *Kantwerken, bijeengebracht uit verschillende verzamelingen*, The Hague 1912

Kuus 1997
S. Kuus, 'Drie aperocken van tieren taijen onder kin-
dergoed uit Wendela Bickers rekeningboek, 1655-
1668', *Kostuum* 1997, pp. 45-62

Laprade 1905
Mme L. de Laprade, *Le Poinct de France et les Centres
Dentellières au XVIIe et XVIIIe Siècles*, Paris 1905

Larensche Kunsthandel 1912
Exhib. cat. Larensche Kunsthandel, *Oude Kant*,
Amsterdam 1912

Lefébure 1887
E. Lefébure, *Broderies et dentelles*, Paris 1887

Lefébure 1904
A. Lefébure, *Dentelles et guipures*, Paris 1904

Lefébure 1912
E. Lefébure, *Les Points de France*, International
Exhibition 1900, Paris. Retrospective Collection. Class
84 - Lace. Report of Monsieur Ernest Lefébure,
Secrétaire du Musée des Arts Decoratifs, Fabriquant de
Dentelles, 5 rue de Castiglione, Paris, translated by
Margaret Taylor Johnston, New York 1912

Lemaire 1904
H. Lemaire, Dessinateur, 'L'Industrie dentellière,
recueil de 1600 documents publié en cent trente plan-
ches. Reproductions de Dentelle Véritable Depuis le
XVIe siècle jusqu'à 1904', *Documents et modèles utilisables
dans toutes les industries d'art*, Paris 1904

Levey 1977
S.M. Levey, 'Lace and Lace-Patterned Silks: some
Comparative Illustrations', V. Gervers (ed.), *Studies in
Textile History*, Royal Ontario Museum, Toronto 1977,
pp. 184-201

Levey 1983
S.M. Levey, *Lace. A History*, London/Leeds 1983

Levey & Payne 1983
S.M. Levey & P.C. Payne, *Le Pompe, 1559. Patterns for
Venetian bobbin lace*, Carlton, Beds., 1983

Levey & Wardle 1994
S.M. Levey & P. Wardle, *The Finishing Touch. Lace in portraits at Frederiksborg*, Det Nationalhistorische Museum
pa Frederiksborg, Denmark 1994

Lotz 1933
A. Lotz, *Bibliographie der Modelbücher*, Leipzig 1933

Luijten er al 1993
G. Luijten er al (ed.), exhib. cat. *Dawn of the Golden Age.
North Netherlandish Art 1580-1620*, Amsterdam
(Rijksmuseum), Zwolle 1993

Lunghi & Pessa
M.D. Lunghi & L. Pessa, *Macramé. L'Arte del pizzo a nodi nei
Paesi Mediterranei*, Genoa 1996

Magué 1930
C. Magué, *Les Dentelles Anciennes*, Paris 1930

Maletot 1927
A. Malotet, *La Dentelle à Valenciennes*, Paris 1927

Mansion House 1913
Exhib. cat. *Catalogue of Exhibition at the Mansion House*,
National Association for the organization of
Handmade Lace in England, London, March 1913

Mariacher et al. 1986
G. Mariacher, er al., L. Purisiol, *Il Merletto di Pellestrina*, Pellestina 1986

Meulen-Nulle 1936
L.M. van der Meulen-Nulle, *Kant*, Amsterdam 1936, 2nd ed. Amsterdam 1957

Meulen-Nulle 1963
L.M. van der Meulen-Nulle, *Lace*, London 1963

Minne-Dansaert 1905
J. Minne-Dansaert, *La Classe des Dentelles et les Broderies. Raport...à l'Exposition universale et internationale de Liège en 1905*

Modes en Dentelles 1983
Exhib. cat. *Modes en Dentelles 1590-1983*, Paris (Musée de la Mode et du costume) 1983

Morris & Hague 1920
F. Morris & M. Hague, *Antique Laces of the American Collectors*, Parts I-IV, New York 1920, Part V, New York 1926

Mottolo Molfino 1984
A. Mottola Molfino, 'Pizzi', *Musei e Gallerie di Milano. Museo Poldi Pezzoli. Arazzi-Tappeti-Tessuti Copti-Pizzi-Ricami-Ventagli*, Milan 1984

Naber 1903
J.W.A. Naber, *Oude en Nieuwe Kantwerken*, Haarlem 1903

Oude Kant 1938
Exhib. cat. *Oude Kant*, Museum Boymans, Rotterdam 1938

Oud-Italiaansche Kunst 1934
Exhib. Cat. *Oud-Italiaansche Kunst in Nederlandsch Bezit*, Stedelijk Museum, Amsterdam 1934

Overloop 1911-1912
E. van Overloop, *Matériaux pour servir à l'histoire de la dentelle en Belgique. Deuxième Serie. Dentelles Anciennes des Musées d'Arts décoratifs et industriels à Bruxelles*, Brussels 1911-1912

Overloop 1914
E. van Overloop, *Matériaux pour servir à l'histoire de la dentelle en Belgique. Troisième Serie. Dentelles anciennes de la collection Alfred Lescure*, Brussels/Paris 1914

Paludan & Hemmer Egeberg 1991
C. Paludan, & L. de Hemmer Egeberg, exhib. cat. *98 Monsterbogen Til Broderi, Knipling og Strikning/98 Patternbooks for Embroidery, Lace and Knitting*, Det Danske Kunstindustrimuseum, Copenhagen 1991

Paludan et al 1991
C. Paludan, P. Wardle & K. Hoffritz, exhib. cat. *Pragt & Poesi. Kniplinger gennemm 400 ar/Pomp & Poetry. Lace through 400 years*, Museum of Decorative Art Copenhagen (Catalogue no. 7) 1991

Parma Armani 1990
E. Parma Armani (et. Al.,ed.), *Il Museo del Pizzo al Tombolo di Rapallo. La manifattura Mario Zennaro 1908-1968*, Genoa 1990

Paulis 1935
L. Paulis, 'Point de France', *Bulletin des Musées Royaux d'Art et d'Histoire* VII (1935), pp.44-46

Paulis 1947(1)
L. Paulis, *Pour Connaître la Dentelle*, Antwerp 1947

Paulis 1947(2)
L. Paulis, *Les Points à l'aiguille Belges*, Musées Royaux d'Art et d'Histoire, Brussels 1947

Poupeye 1910
C. Poupeye, 'Vrouwenkunst op de Brusselsche Tentoonstelling', *De Lelie - Maandelijksch Katholiek Dames-Tijdschrift voor Noord- en Zuid-Nederland* 1 (1910), pp.341-349

Powys 1953
M. Powys, *Lace and Lace-making*, Boston, Mass., 1953

Preysing 1987
M. Gräfin Preysing, *Spitzen*, Museum für Kunst en Kunstgewerbe, Hamburg 1987

Rahir 1920
E. Rahir, *Antoine Watteau. Peintre d'arabesques*, Paris 1920

Riemens 1919
K.J. Riemens, *Esquisse historique de l'enseignement du français en Hollande au XVIe au XIXe siècle*, Leiden 1919

Risselin-Steenebrugen 1956
M. Risselin-Steenebrugen, 'Une Famille de Dentelliers Bruxellois au XVIIIᵉ siècle', *Annales de la Société Royale d'Archéologie de Bruxelles* 48 (1948-55) (1956), pp. 202-237

Risselin-Steenebrugen 1957
M. Risselin-Steenebrugen, 'Caroline d'Halluin, Marchande de Dentelle à Bruxelles au XVIIIᵉ siècle', *Annales de la Société Royale d'Archéologie de Bruxelles* 49 (1956-7) (1957), pp. 1-15

Risselin-Steenebrugen n.d. [c. 1959]
M. Risselin-Steenebrugen *Les dentelles étrangères*, Musées Royaux d'Art et d'Histoire, Brussels, n.d. [c. 1959]

Risselin-Steenebrugen 1961
M. Risselin-Steenebrugen, 'Les débuts de l'industrie dentellière - Martine et Catherine Plantin', *De Gulden Passer* (Antwerp) 39 (1961), pp.77-124

Risselin-Steenebrugen 1965
M. Risselin-Steenebrugen, *Gift van Mevrouw H. Curtiss-Kirstein*, Musées Royaux d'Art et d'Histoire, Brussels 1965

Risselin-Steenebrugen 1956-1966
M. Risselin-Steenebrugen, 'Le Colbertisme et la dentelle de Bruxelles aux fuseaux', *Annales de la Société Royale d'Archéologie de Bruxelles* 51 (1956-1966), pp. 111-121

Risselin-Steenebrugen 1975
M. Risselin-Steenebrugen, 'Essai sur les débuts de l'industrie dentellière à Malines', *Handelingen van de Koninklijke Kring voor Oudheidkunde, Letteren en Kunst van Mechelen* 1975 (1976), pp. 207-217

Risselin-Steenebrugen 1978
M. Risselin-Steenebrugen, 'À propos de la 'dentelle de Gand' et de deux robes princières: évolution de la 'Valenciennes' en Flandre', *Bulletin des Musées Royaux d'Art et d'Histoire* 50 (1978), pp.135-156

Rizzini 1996
M. Rizzini, *Merletti e Ricami dal XVI al XIX secolo. Le collezioni tessili dei Musei Civici de Como*, Como 1996

Rogge 1914
E.M. Rogge, 'La Femme Belge', *De Vrouw en Haar Huis* VIII (1914), pp.392-394

Rogge 1921
E.M. Rogge, 'Oude Kanten', *Nieuwe Rotterdamsche Courant*, 12 maart 1921 Avondblad B

Rogge 1923
E.M. Rogge, De Toegepaste Kunsten in Nederland. Naaldwerk Kantwerk en Handweven, Rotterdam 1923

Rothstein 1990
N.K.A. Rothstein, *Silk Designs of the Eighteenth Century in the Collections of the Victoria and Albert Museum, London*, London 1990

Rothstein 1999
N. Rothstein, 'Fashionable silks and their Influence on the Design of 18th-Century Table Linen', R. Schorter (et. al., ed.), *Leinendamaste. Produktionszentren und Sammlungen*, Abegg-Stiftung, Riggisberg 1999, pp.251-271

Saint-Louis 1910
Exposition Internationale de Saint-Louis, U.S.A. 1904. Section française, Emile Sint, Rapport du Groupe 58, Paris 1906

Schipper-van Lottum 1980
M.G.A. Schipper-van Lottum, *Over Merklappen Gesproken...*, Amsterdam 1980

Schuette 1963
M. Schuette, *Alte Spitzen*, Brunswick 1963 (1st ed. 1913)

Seligman 1923
G. Seligman, 'The Wardrobe of a Princess in 1720', *Bulletin of the Needle and Bobbin Club*, VII no.1 (1923), pp. 2-14

Simeon 1979
M. Simeon, *The History of Lace*, London 1979

Six 1932
J. Six, 'Notes on Early Dutch Lace', *Bulletin of the Needle and Bobbin Club* 16 (1932), pp. 3-16

Smolar-Meynaert & Vincke 1982
A. Smolar-Meynaert & A. Vincke, exhib. cat. *Dentelle de Bruxelles*, Musée du Costume et de la Dentelle, Brussels 1982

Smolar-Meynaert 1991
A. Smolar-Meynaert, exhib. cat. *Dentelles et Têtes Couronnées/Vorstelijke Kant*, Musée du Costume et de la Dentelle de la Ville de Bruxelles, Brussels, 1991

Sonday 1982
M. Sonday, *Lace in the Collection of the Cooper-Hewitt Museum*, Smithsonian Institution, New York 1982

Strinati 1926
R. Strinati, *Il merletti ad ago e la Scuola di Burano*, Rome/Milan 1926

Thornton 1965
P.K. Thornton, *Baroque and Rococo Silks*, London 1965

Trendell 1930
P.G. Trendell, *Guide to the Collection of Lace*, Victoria & Albert Museum, London 1930

Vandenberghe et al 1990
S. Vandenberghe, F. Sorber, L. Van Damme-Ketele & P. Verstraete. *Catalogus van de Kantverzameling, Brugge Guuthusenmuseum*, Bruges 1990

Verhaegen 1902
P. Verhaegen, *La dentelle et la broderie sur tulle*, 2 vols., Brussels 1902

Vlielander Hein 1911
F.E. Vlielander Hein, 'Een opstel over kant', *Het Huis Oud en Nieuw* 9 (1911), pp. 195-225

Wardle 1968
P. Wardle, P., *Victorian Lace*, London 1968, reprinted Carlton:Bedford 1982

Wardle 1969
P. Wardle, 'A late 19th-century lace fan', *Bulletin Museum Boymans-van Beuningen, Rotterdam*, XX (1969), p. 58

Wardle 1983
P. Wardle, 'Needle and Bobbin in Seventeenth-Century Holland',-*Bulletin of the Needle and Bobbin Club* 66 (1983), pp. 3-28

Wardle 1985
P. Wardle, 'Seventeenth-century silk lace in the Rijksmuseum', *Bulletin van het Rijksmuseum* 33 (1985), pp. 207-225

Wardle & De Jong, 1995
P. Wardle & M. de Jong, exhib. cat. *Kant in Mode. Mode in Kant/Lace in Fashion. Fashion in Lace 1815-1914*, Het Kantsalet 1985

Wardle 1989
P. Wardle, 'War and Peace. Lace designs by the Belgian sculptor Isidore de Rudder (1855-1943)', *Bulletin van het Rijksmuseum* 37 (1989), pp. 73-90

Wardle 1992(1)
P. Wardle, exhib. cat. *Nuttig en Nodig. Nederlandse kantopleidingen 1850-1940/Practical and Needful. Dutch Lace Schools 1850-1940*, Het Kantsalet 1992

Wardle 1992(2)
P. Wardle, *Subtle Richness. Lace in the Netherlands 1600-1700*, Rijksmuseum leaflet 5, 1992

Wardle 1995
P. Wardle, '"De belangstelling voor kant wakker te roepen en te onderhouden". De vorming van de kantcollectie van het Rijksmuseum', *Kostuumverzamelingen in beweging*, Nederlandse Kostuumvereniging voor Mode en Streekdracht, Arnhem 1995, pp. 56-64

Wardle 1996
P. Wardle, '"Een toilette kleed met kant". Kanttekening bij de textilia voor de toilettafel in de late zeventiende en achtiende eeuw/Notes on the textiles for the toilet table in the late seventeenth and eighteenth century', *Bulletin van het Rijksmuseum* 44 (1996), pp. 27-38, 71-4

Wardle 1997
P. Wardle, '"Divers necessaries for his Majesty's use and service"; Seamstresses to the Stuart Kings', *Costume. The Journal of the Costume Society* 31 (1997), pp. 16-27

Wardle 1998
P. Wardle, 'Koningin Emma en haar kant/Queen Emma and her lace', *Bulletin van het Rijksmuseum* 46 (1998), pp. 24-58, 102-14

Colophon

This publication appeared in conjunction with the presentation 75 x Lace, 18/03 - 20/08/2000, at the Rijksmuseum, Amsterdam

Author:
Patricia Wardle

Editor:
Bianca M. du Mortier

Photography:
Department of Photography, Rijksmuseum: Madeleine ter Kuile and Peter Mookhoek, with the exception of the photographs listed in the photo credits

Catalogue design:
Frank de Wit, Cactus, Raalte

Printing:
Waanders Printers, Zwolle

© 2000 Uitgeverij Waanders b.v., Zwolle
Rijksmuseum, Amsterdam

ISBN 90 400 9448 9

NUGI 926, 911

Cover: Catalogue no. 7, detail
Frontispiece: Catalogue no. 36, detail

Photo credits

Amsterdam, Amsterdams Historisch Museum, 16b

Apeldoorn, Paleis Het Loo, on loan from Stichting Historische Verzamelingen van het Huis Oranje-Nassau, photo A.A.W. Meine Jansen, 21a

Brussels, Copyright IRPA-KIK, Brussels, 47a, 58a

Copenhagen, Det Danske Kunstindustrimuseum, photo Ole Woldbye, 6a

London, V & A Picture Library, 62a

New York, Cooper Hewitt, National Design Museum, 16a

Rotterdam, Atlas van Stolk, 53a

Rotterdam, Museum Boijmans Van Beuningen, 20a

Paris, Private collection, 11a

Vienna, Österreichisches Museum für Angewandte Kunst, 72a

Every effort has been made to apprise all institutions and other concerned parties of the publication of photographic material. Any unintentional oversight may be communicated to the Rijksmuseum, Amsterdam (Exhibition Office).

RIJKSMUSEUM
1800 2000
AMSTERDAM